D1304896

EDUCATION IN SCOTLAND

World Education Series

General Editors: Michael D. Stephens,
MA, MEd, PhD, FRGS

Gordon W. Roderick,
BSc, MA, PhD, MInst P,
University of Liverpool

Education in
Scotland

IAN R. FINDLAY, MA, MEd
Senior Lecturer in Education
Aberdeen College of Education

DAVID & CHARLES   *Newton Abbot*
ARCHON BOOKS   *Hamden, Connecticut*

LA
652
· F56

This edition first published in 1973 in Great Britain by
David & Charles (Holdings) Limited, Newton Abbot, Devon,
and in the United States by Archon Books, Hamden,
Connecticut, 06514

ISBN 0 7153 5744 1 (Great Britain)
ISBN 0 208 01309 1 (United States)

To my wife

Set in eleven on thirteen point Imprint
and printed in Great Britain
by Latimer Trend & Company Limited Plymouth

Contents

I

Historical Development of Scottish Education

AD 563–1560

THE non-Scot, generally speaking, seems to have an inborn conviction about the high quality of Scottish education. The image may not stand up to close examination, but there is no doubt that the provision of education in Scotland has had a 'lang pedigree'.

St Columba's arrival in Scotland in 563 can be taken as a starting point. Iona became the base from which, during six centuries, monasteries of the Celtic church were founded all over Scotland, and through the seminaries attached to some of these teaching was provided—at first for monks only, and later (from approximately the seventh century) for boys in the surrounding districts. Iona, in fact, became something of an international centre, receiving students from England, Ireland and Scandinavia. Although little is known about its history after the first half of the eighth century, it is likely that it continued as a place of learning until well into the eleventh century. The curriculum probably centred on religion, the ancient languages, sacred manuscripts, the elements of poetic metre and a little astronomy. This was not the total educational activity of the monastery, of course, since agriculture, trades and crafts were almost inevitably practised and taught.

In the late eleventh century began the period of transition from the Celtic to the Roman form of Christianity in Scotland. This brought new and extensive cultural links with Europe, the setting up of a parish and diocesan system (significant in post-Reformation educational development) and the growth of a cathedral-centred education. From the thirteenth century onwards the Dominican order also provided conventual schools (ie convent schools for the training of novices), provincial seminaries and *studia generalia*—the embryo of the later universities. Thus evolved a pattern of cathedral schools, abbey schools, collegiate schools, parish schools, and 'song schools' for choristers. Each town in Scotland was equipped with these schools by 1500, and many of them became the grammar schools of a later period.

Universities have had great influence over the tradition and development of Scottish education, and Scots have placed, and continue to place, a high value on them. But until the fifteenth century there was no Scottish university. For 300 years Scots went south to Oxford, and in greater numbers to the Continental universities, especially to Paris and Bologna: in the second half of the fourteenth century, for instance, about 100 Scots studied in England and about 400 on the Continent. As a result of this exodus Scottish educational traditions have a greater affinity with European than with English patterns. A European outlook is no new thing in Scotland.

In the fifteenth century, three Scottish universities were founded (St Andrew's 1411, Glasgow 1450, Aberdeen 1494), offering mainly, though not exclusively, a form of general education which was preparatory to that of the faculties of the older universities in England and the Continent.

In 1496 an Act provided for the education, from the age of eight or nine years, of the eldest sons of the ruling barons, the object being the production of a class of lawyers to administer justice. This was the first European statute designed to implement some form of compulsory education, though the section of the population aimed at was, of course, limited by sex and class, and the needs of the time.

1560–1803

The Protestant Reformation of the mid-sixteenth century was crucial for the development of Scottish education. To suggest, however, that education was not provided before this is, as we

have seen, quite mistaken. In fact the Roman church in the 1540s
and 1550s was clearly accepting the challenge of the Protestant
reformers and putting its educational house in order. By 1560,
however, a situation had come about, through the intervention
of Elizabeth of England and the expulsion of French and
Catholic influences from Scotland, in which it was possible for
the new Protestant church to set up a new system, which included
strong and farsighted emphasis on education. The proposed
national system of education for Scotland was set forth in the
first of two *Books of Discipline*, the authors being (in twentieth-
century educational jargon) 'the Knox Committee', that is,
John Knox the great Protestant reformer and five colleagues.
This was a well co-ordinated plan, the spirit of which was to
dominate Scottish education for over three centuries until the
eventual formation of a state system. In fact subsequent educational legislation could be described as repeated attempts to
come ever closer to the original reformers' aims, usually summed
up as 'a school in every parish'.

Briefly, the intention was to achieve the following:

For 5–8 years: elementary schools in country parishes, teaching reading and elements of the Catechism, the
teacher to be the reader or minister of the
parish. The twin aims of 'literacy and godli-
ness' were to be basic.

For 8–12 years: grammar schools in 'towns of any repute', for
the teaching of Latin grammar.

For 12–16 years: high schools (or colleges) 'in important towns'
(possibly diocesan centres) for the teaching of
Latin, Greek, logic and rhetoric.

For 16–19 years: a three-year Arts course at university.

For 19–24 years: a five-year medicine, law or divinity course—
the ultimate professional preparation.

Necessary comments on this system:

1. Its total aim was nothing less than the moral good of the
individual and his service to the community.

2. The reformers had no truck with distinctions between rich
and poor.

3. Promotion from one stage to the next was to depend on ability—this is the root of the Scottish tradition of 'democratic meritocracy'. Lack of money never closed the door of opportunity, only lack of ability, and, of course, a narrowly academic ability. From this derive both the best and the worst in the Scottish educational tradition.

4. Finance was to come from confiscated lands of the Roman church, but in the event this did not happen as they were appropriated largely by the nobility.

5. The universities' part in this scheme was to provide a very broad, general upper 'secondary' education before the real university course began at the age of nineteen. In later centuries the bright scholar did in fact go straight from parish school (or via a short grammar-school course) to university in his mid-teens. Traditions of postponement of specialisation in the Scottish school stem from this pattern.

6. Parliament rejected the scheme but because of the long involvement of the Scottish church in education ever since, it has acted as a blueprint for development nevertheless.

In the period from the seventeenth to the nineteenth centuries, therefore, there was a reasonably continuous expansion of parish and burgh schools, supplemented from the early 1700s by private provision. After 1803 control passed slowly from church to state, but the complete transfer was a late nineteenth-century occurrence.

Legislation in the seventeenth century indicates something of the progress of the Scottish parish school (not the burgh school). Acts of 1616, 1633 and 1646 represent continual attempts to give a firm basis to the system by requiring the heritors* of every parish to provide for a school, a schoolmaster and his salary. They were not very successful, especially in the Highland region, understandably, where not only was clan warfare endemic but there was also great opposition to the official attempt to stamp out the indigenous Celtic culture and language. However, the Act of 1696 'for the Settling of Schools' was much more effective, making it a legal obligation on the heritors of the parish

* The local landowners, varying from some 3 to 30 in number according to region and system of land distribution, ie whether large estates or small holdings.

to provide school, schoolmaster and salary—with the threat that, should they fail to do so, commissioners of supply were to be directed to do the job and charge the expense to the heritors. In addition, if any heritor fell into arrears with payment, he was after a fixed time to be required to pay double.

Throughout the seventeenth century the Scottish church played a very large part in the promotion of schooling: through the direct action of its presbyteries in planting rural schools, through its pressure upon the Scottish Parliament to improve burgh schooling, and by direct financial subsidy where needed. It also insisted on controlling most strictly the appointment of teachers (who had to sign the Confession of Faith) and on the right to inspect the schools.

The eighteenth century threw up no memorable educational legislation, which is all the more surprising when one considers that between 1700 and 1800 Scotland was changing from a poor agricultural country to a relatively industrialised society, with all that is implied in educational need. Not until 1803 did a major Act try to meet the situation. As for the parish school system, the century was characterised by a long struggle on the part of church presbyteries to force parish heritors to meet their legal obligations over school provision.

Burgh schools in the seventeenth and eighteenth centuries provided the 'secondary' education (sense as under comment 5 on p 12) of the age. In the smaller towns they combined this with elementary education in English, writing and arithmetic—the famous Scottish 'three Rs'—but in the larger centres elementary education to the age of nine years was left in the hands of separate schools for reading and writing. In burgh schools geographically close to a university, much emphasis was placed on the classical/mathematical curriculum leading to university, to the virtual exclusion of other subjects—social, recreational or practical—while in the more remote centres some at least of the subjects familiar in a modern curriculum were added. School hours were very long, but over the years were made shorter; instruction tended to be on a departmental basis, and teachers were better qualified than those of the parish schools in that rather less than half were graduates and about three-quarters had been to university. Staff appointments differed from the church-controlled parish schools in that the town council made the decision, subject to church approval in the form of examination by a six-man commission of local university professors.

It is broadly true of the whole of this period that (a) parish schools in certain instances developed a secondary/pre-university function, and (b) that burgh schools in some cases had an elementary/preparatory stage prior to secondary teaching. Each of these patterns has lasted long in Scotland in given areas (eg the all-age primary/junior secondary of the 1940s to 1960s, typical of the rural area, and the now dwindling number of primary departments in the old grammar and burgh schools). But both parish and burgh school laid the foundations of modern primary and secondary schooling respectively.

One other important aspect of schooling before the 1803 Act was the provision of voluntary schools in the eighteenth century (and indeed, with changing emphasis but decreasing effectiveness, into the industrial nineteenth century) by the SSPCK (Society in Scotland for Propagating Christian Knowledge). Their main drive was to establish schools in the parishes of the Highlands for the rooting out of 'error, idolatry, superstition and ignorance', but because of the troubled political history of the Highlands—the two Jacobite rebellions, the subsequent 'pacification' and the terrible cruelty of the enforced clearance of Highlanders in the late eighteenth century from land required for sheep farming—this was not too successful. Nevertheless, in the period up to 1803 the SSPCK performed a valuable function in filling the holes in school provision until the state took over. It developed technical and local craft education at the turn of the century to meet the industrial situation, but its influence, where schools were established, was unfortunately detrimental to Gaelic culture and language, and was intended to be.

1803–1872

The 1803 Act was the first major development of the Scottish educational situation from the 1696 position, made necessary by the fact that Scotland was rapidly becoming an industrial society; schooling was inadequate to meet the population situation in large parishes, illiteracy was widespread, and teaching unattractive as an occupation. The main points of the Act are listed below.

1. It improved to some extent the provision of teachers' salaries.
2. It improved minimum standards for the housing of teachers in part payment of salaries.
3. It restated in detail the control of the Church of Scotland over the appointment of teachers—this in the 1803 situation should be seen as the best and only way of ensuring minimum standards of suitability at that time.
4. It gave powers to parish heritors to establish 'side schools', that is, an additional school in those parishes where one was insufficient. Even this did not ensure adequate provision in the nineteenth century, so that the church itself had also to establish its own schools.

The general effect of this Act was, strangely enough, not an increase in church power, but the beginning of sixty-nine years of struggle between the church and the secular money-source, the heritors of the parish, who were the forerunners of the modern ratepayers.

Industrialisation in Scotland between 1803 and 1872 was rapid, especially in Glasgow, Clydeside and the central belt, where there was an increase in population from about 84,000 to just under half a million in this period. In the absence of strong governmental planning, therefore, schools were just not available for more than a fraction of school-age children, the figure in Glasgow particularly being about 40 per cent by the end of the period. The Highlands also were short of schools, in view of the difficulty of providing for a sparsely populated area, the lack of any dynamic drive for education from the centre, and official reluctance to cater for education in the Gaelic language. The problem in the industrial areas of the south-west was intensified by the continuous influx of Irish immigrants and the creation of a large Roman Catholic segment of the population which demanded its own, separate school provision. This legacy has remained with the west of Scotland until the present day (it is also present in a less obvious form in other urban areas), a similar if less intense segregation than that evident in twentieth-century Northern Ireland where there are separate systems for the two major church groups.

The result of all this was that in both town and rural areas very few of the limited number attending school stayed more than five years or so. However, redeeming features of the social scene were to be found. Infant school voluntary societies did provide schooling for some children from the age of three; private industrialists such as Robert Owen (who set up a pioneer social welfare scheme in New Lanark with much emphasis on a programme of education surprisingly liberal for the time) also played their part. The state, on the other hand, took little part in the financing of schools in the early part of this period, although giving encouragement to voluntary provision, but in the 1830s and 1840s began to give a little assistance for buildings and upkeep of schools. This growing involvement culminated in the recommendation of the Argyll Commission in 1867 (to be mentioned again later) that a rate should be levied for education, a financial move which laid the foundation for the post-1872 period of state-financed education. Despite continual attempts to persuade the government to take planning initiative and responsibility, this did not happen for the greater part of the nineteenth century. Instead, a school system designed for the conditions of the seventeenth and eighteenth centuries (and full of holes even then) functioned, but it did not meet society's needs in the Industrial Revolution era.

The parish schools continued much as before, increased inadequately in number by the 1803 Act and doing a reasonable job of elementary education (in the nineteenth-century understanding of the phrase) for as many as they could reach; this lasted until the state came to the rescue and set about the task of building a national network of elementary schools for all, in the last quarter of the century. The parish-school curriculum, which provides the traditional image of Scottish education, consisted of the familiar reading, writing, arithmetic, and of course religion—

'four Rs' in fact. At this time it was very common for the village 'dominie', or schoolmaster, himself probably the past recipient of university education in whole or part, to give much time to the 'lad o' pairts', the academically bright pupil, and to continue instructing him to the age of fourteen or sixteen at which time he might well leave for his studies in one of the four universities. The very name 'dominie' carries with it an aura of rural respect for education, and the phrase 'lad o' pairts' has strong associations of the Scottish tradition of unlimited access to education for the academically able from poor origins.

The north-east of Scotland deserves special mention as the strongest bulwark of this essentially Scottish tradition, since, because of the existence of a special fund called the Dick Bequest, local parish schoolmasters were financed and encouraged to upgrade their qualifications. This resulted in a high proportion of able teachers, and had its effect upon the nature of the student body in the University of Aberdeen, containing as it did a large number of country boys straight from extended parish schooling as opposed to burgh schooling. Such effective parish schools in some cases have developed into modern secondary centres.

In the realm of secondary schooling proper, burgh schools also tended to continue as before, the curriculum in some cases going beyond university-oriented studies, but still with a largely classical emphasis. These had in fact been joined on the educational stage from the 1760s onwards by a new kind of school foundation known as the 'academy', formed in reaction to the narrowness of the burgh school curriculum, and giving more time to scientific, commercial and practical subjects. Academies continued to be founded into the 1830s: their initial high standard of staffing, buildings and internal organisation had a good effect on the older burgh schools and their curriculum, and as evangelistic zeal waned in the later nineteenth century the two kinds of school came together (physically in some cases) to provide a wide basis of Scottish academic secondary schooling. Most of these, as a combined group, became the senior secondaries of the 1940s.

B

In the area of voluntary or non-parish-based schooling, the
SSPCK, as indicated earlier, continued to be active, but with a
falling off of activity towards the 1860s and 70s. But a development characteristic of the nineteenth century was the foundation
of denominational schools by the various churches. In this
respect the Scottish educational scene began to take on some of
the character of that south of the border; but these schools could
not be described as the mainstream of Scottish educational
tradition. They were essentially an attempt to re-establish a
church control of education that was gradually being lost to the
secular authorities originally set up by the church itself. But the
Church of Scotland also moved into the field for the same reason
as the SSPCK, in the Highlands and Islands for example,
where 'assembly schools' were established. Also, in the towns,
'sessional schools' maintained by the Scottish church helped
to deal with the vast industrial problem mentioned earlier—
special effort being made in Glasgow where the need was
greatest. These must be commended as determined efforts and
of great assistance to school provision before state intervention
in 1872. The Free Church of Scotland (the result of the Disruption of the Church of Scotland in 1843) also provided schools,
as did also the Roman Catholic and Scottish Episcopal churches.
The extent of this provision will be evident in the statistics of
the Argyll Commission Report of 1867 referred to later in this
chapter.

In Scotland, as in England, it is difficult to get a clear picture
of education in the nineteenth century because of the many
agencies participating. Private adventure schools, for instance,
grew to great numbers, mostly bad and run by unqualified
people, but throwing up one or two good secondary foundations
of high repute. In addition, there were endowed foundations or
'hospitals', factory, works and industrial schools of various kinds,
infant schools and Gaelic society schools in the Highlands. But
in the 1860s two things were plain: firstly the situation was a
scandalously disorganised one for a modern industrial society,
and secondly, both secondary and elementary schooling were
inadequate. Unfortunately, secondary schooling was not given

new life by the 1872 Act, which concentrated on the reorgnisa-
tion of schooling at elementary level.

Growing influence of the state   Before considering the
1872 Act, however, it would be useful to look at the ways in
which the state moved into Scottish education in the nineteenth
century. Firstly, by the Act of 1838, an attempt was made to
found additional 'Parliamentary schools' to patch up the still
existing holes in school provision. This gave some help at least
in the following thirty-four years. The 1861 Act was effective,
however, since it altered certain legislation on parish and burgh
schools, and particularly the whole basis of appointment of
teachers. The power of teacher examination was removed from
the presbyteries, and placed in the hands of four university
boards of professors from arts and divinity faculties, with help
from Her Majesty's Inspectors of Schools where necessary. The
teachers 'oath' was no longer to be the positive Confession of
Faith, but a declaration promising to teach nothing against the
faith, a more negative emphasis. Church participation was
reduced to the power of complaint—effectively a removal of
power altogether. The age of secular control in Scottish state
education had dawned.

Financially, the first government grants came to Scottish
education simultaneously with those in England in 1833, but
were not used until a little later for the purposes of building more
schools or for the implementation of teacher training. 1846 saw
the extension of the grant to school equipment, maintenance of
teachers' housing and the pupil-teacher system, and the 1850s
the beginning of grants (from departments of science and art set
up as a result of concern over foreign industrial competition)
for the development of these two subjects in secondary schools.

The new actor on the educational stage, the HMI (Her
Majesty's Inspector), has already been mentioned. The first
Inspectors were appointed in 1840, on a strictly denominational
basis (naturally enough in the context of the imminent Disruption
of the Church of Scotland and of the complex pattern of
denominational schools), a system which lasted until the introduction of a purely state pattern in 1872. Their task was to report

to the Committee of Council (a special committee of the Privy Council set up in 1839 to deal with educational matters) on every aspect of schooling, and this they did with increasingly thorough coverage of the country throughout the three 'denominational decades'. The system had its critics and its abuses: strained relations with teachers; lessons taught *ad nauseam* in preparation for the unexpected visit; an early warning system manned by school pupils suitably positioned or perhaps by suspiciously hospitable Highland ferrymen who might send urgent messages to the local dominie while detaining the visiting gentleman in as pleasant a way as possible; charges of 'graduate inexperience' against HMIs, and so on. But the system, with all its faults, was a decided improvement on the previous half-hearted presbytery visitation.

Another important factor affecting the 'final run-in' to the 1872 Act was the Revised Code. In 1860 an Education Code was drawn up, bringing together all previous measures initiated by the Committee of Council in respect of schooling, but it applied to Britain as a whole and was thus not entirely appropriate to the distinctive Scottish parish school situation. In 1862 this was superseded by the Revised Code, effective from 1864, which introduced a system of payment by results. This was destined to restrict the curricular growth of Scottish education for a long time to come, and could be unequivocally condemned as one of the 'bad moves' in Scottish educational history. The essence of this system was the giving of grants to schools on the basis of such factors as unbroken attendance for whole school years by individual children, and subject proficiency for six-year-olds and over. The corollary was withdrawal of grants for bad results. A compromise which developed retained the individual examination but not the individual grant on a result basis—the grant being to the class. The system led to greater attention to individual attainment but also to a meaningless mechanical grind of preparation for assessment rather than learning. The fine tradition of preparing the bright lad in the parish school for the university suffered because of the need to concentrate on bread-and-butter teaching.

Further education   In the field of adult education, this period saw the slow growth of evening classes catering for literacy and basic attainments on the whole, and, largely from the 1820s onwards, of Mechanics' Institutes—the purposes of which were many and varied, but often connected with skill improvement for the industrial artisan. Technical Colleges grew out of the more successful urban Institutes and provided the nuclei of the future Central Institutions—and, of course, in our own time, of some new universities.

Teacher training as a part of the education system in Scotland dates from 1837, when a college in Dundas Vale, based on the previous work of the infant school founded by David Stow of the Glasgow Education Society, was opened and became the first British teachers' college. Further teacher training was for the next sixty or seventy years undertaken by colleges under the supervision of the various church denominations. A transitional phase towards the modern non-denominational position was the sixty-year period of the pupil-teacher system in force from 1846, in which selected thirteen-year-olds served a period of five years combined teacher training and secondary schooling, leading to the possibility of competing for scholarship-financed training at a college. (This system of teacher training is non-existent now in Scotland, and is obsolescent in countries striving for uniform teachers' status in a unified education system.) By the time of the 1872 Act, teachers in Scotland had, however, only moved one-third of the way to the goal of an entirely certificated profession. The universities took no part in teacher training. This is a sector in which Scottish universities have been involved only briefly at the turn of the twentieth century. Scottish colleges are still regional bodies for the training/education of all teachers. The development of the theme of teacher training after 1872 will be taken up in the next section of this chapter.

In the earlier years of this period each university tended to serve regional rather than national purposes, and to hold on to its own traditional lecture system. Their very existence encouraged high standards in the preceding schooling, and their production of more graduates than could fill posts in law, medicine or the ministry ensured a good supply of second-choice entrants into teaching, though it may be questioned whether this did anything for the status of the teaching profession. There was a good deal of dissatisfaction, however, with standards of university teaching, but in spite of it many young people gave up a great deal, travelled long distances and suffered poor lodgings and hardship in order to study and graduate. Curricula in law, medicine and divinity in the earlier nineteenth century were on the whole unchanged since the eighteenth, but the existence of colourful rival medical and surgical schools enlivened the university towns. In the case of divinity the Disruption of the Scottish church did not in the long run cause separate university provision, although this was proposed in the 1840s.

In the sphere of legislation, the 1826 Act made recommendations for the reorganisation of the universities, which, to cut a complex story short, were for the most part put into effect by the Act of 1858. The Act gave governmental control of the university to its Senate and created two new university bodies, the Court and the General Council—the first of which was to be concerned with finance and the question of appeals against Senate decisions, the second (including the Chancellor, the Court and all qualified graduates and staff) with elections and general welfare. Thus the modern autonomy of the university came into being, and Edinburgh threw off the restrictions of town control, which it alone had suffered in the past. The office of Rector was retained, as a kind of safeguard for the students' interests, its value depending on the particular incumbent. There was no insistence (though it was needed) on minimal university entrance standards, but three-year Arts degrees became accepted, with an Honours MA (a specialist four-year degree) in selected fields. Encouragement was given to the universities to form a federated collegiate national institution but nothing came of this—probably because of the independent regional traditions of the various universities. By 1872, the Scottish universities had given evidence of a concern both with teaching and research, and it could be said that neither was neglected at the expense of the other. The modern Scottish University in its essentials, therefore, emerged by the end of the period preceding compulsory education.

The Argyll Commission   To complete the account of this period, the findings of the Argyll Commission (1864–67) must be mentioned. Every aspect of existing schooling was covered, and evidence and statistics amassed from every possible source. It produced a picture of high average absenteeism, but a better standard of schooling in the rural than in the urban areas, and recommended standards of cost, size, space, as well as of level of instruction and so on. The school provision pattern uncovered was:

519	Church of Scotland schools
617	Free Church schools
74	Episcopal schools
61	Roman Catholic schools
202	SSPCK schools
1,100	parish schools
50	burgh schools
23	academies

This, of course, does not include higher or further education, which lay outside the Commissions brief.

Their recommendations were:

1. That a Board of Education should be set up centrally, with responsibility for building, accommodation and finance— this would be a composite body with members from the towns, the churches and the universities. The Board was to deal with administrative matters and not policy.

2. That public schools (ie state schools and not public schools in the English sense) should be established and supported by the levying of a rate—to fill existing gaps and supplement the provision already made.

3. That there should be annual inspection, despite objections to the Revised Code.

4. That there should be grants for new building.

5. That school endowments should be revised and rationalised.

6. That there should be provision for superannuation and insurance schemes for teachers.

7. That three-tier schooling should be introduced: elementary to age 9, intermediate to age 13 and higher to age 17, the

last divided into an arts and science line—a scheme extra-
ordinarily like some modern proposals for a three-tier
comprehensive system and unusually advanced for its time.

All this led to the famous Act with which we begin the last
part of the story, the Education Act of 1872.

1872–1972

The clearest way to understand the last hundred years' development in Scottish education is to study the main areas of educational evolution, with some necessary cross references.

Administration   The main purpose of the 1872 Act was to
establish a state system of elementary education, and to make this
compulsory from the ages of five to thirteen. Thus Scottish
education shared with English a starting age unusual still throughout the world, one recommended as desirable in the sixteenth-
century 'blueprint', Knox's first *Book of Discipline*, but which
was not typical in the years from the Reformation to the 1707
Union. In this period a starting age of seven was usual in
Scottish rural areas, as in Scandinavia, but five became a standard starting age with the growth of an industrialised society in
the eighteenth century. 'Elementary education' included both
parish and, to some extent, burgh schools, while opportunity
was given for the absorption of denominational schools, a chance
taken by some, but not by Roman Catholic or Episcopal schools
until the Act of 1918. Religious education was, in fact, safe-
guarded by conscience clauses in the Act.

The Act established a system of nearly 1,000 school boards,
this being also the number of parishes and burghs in Scotland.
These school boards, of 5–15 members, were given the supervision of all facets of schooling, with a proposed finance system
of government grant, local rate and fees, and a duty of appointing .
teachers, this last point being a natural progression from an Act
of 1861 which had transferred control of appointments from
church presbyteries to the universities. But this system, despite
its undoubted success in expanding school provision in the
1880s and 1890s and in the period before World War I, depended
on too many separate units for effectiveness, and in 1918 the

1,000 school boards gave way to 38 county and city authorities, designed specifically for *ad hoc* educational administration. These were criticised for their narrow outlook and from 1929 the present system of educational control vested in a general-purpose county/town council, acting through its education committee and sub-committees, became the national pattern.

Centrally (which unfortunately meant London!) a 'Scotch Education Department' was set up. Such a travesty of a name could only have been perpetrated in England! Fortunately, in 1918 this properly became the Scottish Education Department—halfway through seventy years of dour struggle by Scots to drag its offices back to Edinburgh. Until 1878 the SED in London worked with a Board in Edinburgh, but from 1878 to 1885 the London Committee of Privy Council on Education catered for the whole United Kingdom. In 1885 a Secretary for Scotland was appointed with powers also as Vice-President of the Scotch Education Department. This situation obtained until 1939, power being effectively in the hands of the Secretary alone after World War I. In 1926, the Secretary became, as he is now, Secretary of State for Scotland, and from 1939 has been directly responsible for the SED from his office in Edinburgh.

Finance, from being based on voluntary sources before the 1872 Act, became, in the late nineteenth century, a complex business of private payments, local subsidies and endowments, and central exchequer grants. This was rationalised in 1908, as an Education (Scotland) Fund to be dispensed by the Scotch Education Department which in 1918 took control of all money from Parliament for Scottish education. In 1958, general legislation changed this to the present government-local authority partnership which, with present-day administration generally, will be described in the following chapter.

Outline of legislation, 1872 to present day   We have seen already the main points of the 1872 Act. Concentrating as it did on elementary education, it left the problems of secondary provision to be solved at a later date, in an age when industrial needs were making wider technical schooling necessary as well as traditional academic curricula.

The following are the legislative bare bones of the last hundred years:

1878 and 1882: Inspection imposed on *Higher Class schools* (five-year burgh, grammar, high and academy institutions); many endowed institutions became secondary schools.

1883: Leaving age raised to 14, with permitted half-time education 10–14.

1889: County councils established and *elementary schooling partially free* (three years later an extra grant was made available for secondary schooling).

1890: End of payment by results. Financial assistance provided for *special schools* for the blind and deaf mutes.

1898: Superannuation scheme introduced for elementary school teachers.

1899: *Advanced departments* (two-years' post-elementary schooling based on merit certificate) introduced.

1901: Leaving age fully established as 14.

The term *primary* takes the place of *elementary*, ie the theoretical entitlement of all children to two consecutive stages of education established. The nineteenth-century position was that two systems of two kinds (totally elementary, and elementary/secondary) existed in parallel (the 1944 Act accomplished this change for England).

1903: *Supplementary courses* replaced 'advanced departments' of 1899 vintage. From 1923–36 these were known as *Advanced Division*, providing a combined general and vocational course.

1906: School boards to have a legal duty to provide for all handicapped children in cases where parents unable to do so.

1908: Provision for medical supervision and meals permitted (social welfare emerges in school).

Obligation placed upon local authority to provide continuation classes for all (14–17) who wished to attend. These developed up to World War I.

No change proposed in school board pattern of administration by Liberal Government, despite much debate

over the degree of reforming zeal that might be expected
from 1,000 small authorities.

Education (Scotland) Fund established to simplify and
centralise finance.

Intermediate education clarified as a concept between
elementary and secondary, leading to Intermediate Certificate. This became regarded as halfway stage to Higher
Leaving Certificate.

Assistance given to pupils with travel, books, equipment,
lodgings and hostels.

Special arrangements made for the schooling of the
handicapped.

Right of appeal allowed to teachers in case of dismissal.

Superannuation schemes for teachers extended from
elementary to all schools.

Government grant to universities substantially increased.

1913: Authorities compelled to provide medical attention free
for all schoolchildren.

1918: Attempt to reorganise the 'whole fabric of the Scottish
educational system outside the universities'.

Education Boards superseded by 38 Education Authorities (these *ad hoc* authorities were replaced by 35 Education Committees of Counties in 1929).

School management committees set up to offset remote-
ness of the new education authorities—but their powers
were severely limited.

Leaving age to be raised to 15; date unspecified. (This did
not in fact happen, because of the economic difficulties of
1920s and 30s.)

Proposed compulsory further education 15–18. This good
proposal, contemporary with the effective example of
Germany's *Berufschule* (vocational school), again did not
materialise because of economic pressures.

Name of SED changed from 'Scotch' to 'Scottish'.

Education authorities instructed to set up advisory
councils within three months. Nothing resulted, for
reasons as before.

Voluntary schools to be given public financial support and the chance to transfer to the education authority, with denominational status guaranteed. Most schools did transfer. This was a highly successful solution of the Church/State problem common to most countries.

Power given to set up *nursery schools*. Economic situation of 1920s ruined attempts.

Move to unify the education system by placing secondary schools under the same authorities as primary schools.

Encouragement to open centres for *day-release training* at post-15 age; ie technical education to be *after* liberal education, not *within* it (the low status of handwork in Scottish secondary schooling stems from this).

Authorities empowered to pay fees and grant bursaries to the able as far as university.

Previous permissive legislation (1908) on travel, lodging grants and provision of hostels reinforced. So originated the now familiar problem of the separation of Highland and rural children from the family at age of 12.

Employment of children under 13 during school hours, and of children over 13 engaged on part-time further education, forbidden.

Teachers further protected from dismissal by new regulations stating the minimum time interval for the submitting of a motion of dismissal to the education committee, and the requirement of a quorum for a committee meeting.

1930: Education authorities given power to issue free school milk.
1936: (following the Hadow Report recommendations of 1926) Recognition that all children over 12 should be in some form of secondary school. Provision for raising leaving age to 15 in September 1939 (outbreak of war stopped this but 14–15 curriculum problem emerges).

Appearance of modern bipartite division into *junior secondary* and *senior secondary*. Proposals for Junior Leaving Certificate never implemented, but the 5/3 year secondary pattern remained.

Teachers to have right of appeal to the Secretary of State against dismissal.

1945: 'Education according to age, ability and aptitude' as objective.

Secondary education for all, free and compulsory, with *leaving age 15 and intention of raising it to 16 as soon as possible.* System of Senior (academic) and Junior (non-academic) secondaries.

Appointment of a separate Director of Education now legally necessary. The office had been combined hitherto with that of County Clerk.

Secretary of State permitted to finance *educational research.*

Nursery schools to be established by authorities where there was sufficient demand.

Authorities to provide medical inspection for all children. A parent must submit his child to examination, but need not accept treatment.

Provision of milk and meals for all children to be compulsory.

Authorities to provide transport for children living beyond walking distance from school (2 miles age 5–8, 3 miles over age 8).

Provision for 'pupils requiring special educational treatment' rationalised—trend to centralisation.

Marriage disqualification for women teachers abolished.

1942 government circular recommending the formation of local authority Youth Services; provision for state aid to deserving voluntary youth organisations.

Independent schools to be placed on register for state inspection.

Authorities to provide facilities for recreation, social and physical training *for all children.*

Proposal to establish Junior Colleges for day release of all the 15–18 group not in full-time secondary education. This faded eventually, preference being given to the objective of 16 years as the school-leaving age.

1946: Reorganisation of the educational endowment system.

Fines to be imposed on parents contravening child employment legislation.

Further confirmation of 1945 state support for the Youth Service and the advisability of assisting voluntary youth organisations.

Religious education not to be discontinued without a mandate from electors.

Authorities to choose between maintaining a separate Youth Employment Service or relying on the Ministry of Labour.

1962: Further consolidation on the lines of 1946.

1963: Education committees given power to co-opt teachers.

The evolution of the school system, 1872–1972   The 1872 Act created *Higher Class* five-year academic secondary schools, a category including burgh, grammar, high and later academy institutions. *Higher Grade* three-year science and commercial schools became a second category in 1899, and in the same year *Advanced departments* became a form of post-elementary (and potentially Higher Grade) schooling. From 1903 Advanced departments became *Supplementary courses* of two years, based on a 'qualifying examination' (an academic hurdle destined to cause both cramming and criticism in the next eighteen years). In 1921 SED Circular 44 abolished the 'qualifying' and introduced local 'promotion' examination schemes (mainly English and arithmetic) which were not, however, much better in their effect on elementary schooling. 1923 saw Supplementary courses changed into *Advanced divisions* (into which the promotion schemes fed pupils from 1924), leading to Day School Certificate (Lower) in two years, and Day School Certificate (Higher) in three years. Meanwhile, secondary five-year courses led to the Higher Leaving Certificate which had been introduced in 1888, this being the only truly 'secondary' education. In 1923 also appeared (a) the Day Schools Code and (b) the Secondary Schools Regulations to control the resultant two levels of schooling. In 1936, all post-primary education became known as secondary for the 12–15 age range, and the situation became one of bipartite schooling leading to the Higher or the Junior Leaving Certificate after five or three years. In 1945 two categories of senior and junior secondary schools were established (many rural secondaries contained both sets of children). In 1962, the tendency for three-year secondaries to 'grow' a fourth year was encouraged by the introduction of the Ordinary Grade Certificate at age 16. This was also a potential stepping stone towards Higher Leaving Certificate, now called Scottish Certificate of Education Higher Grade. In 1965, Government Circular 600 required reorganisation towards a comprehensive school secondary structure, and this is the situation in the 70s.

Further Education   The story of Further Education has to some extent been told in the above 'legislative skeleton' (pp 26–30). The nineteenth century saw the introduction of government financial backing for post-compulsory education, rationalised under the Scotch Education Department in 1897 and categorised in 1901 as (a) continued elementary, (b) elementary technical, (c) three- or four-year technical, (d) non-vocational. From this Code grew the famous central institutions such as the Royal College of Science and Technology in Glasgow and the Heriot Watt College in Edinburgh—both now of university status. As indicated in the list above, 1908, 1918 and 1945 saw the progressive introduction of part-time post-schooling for the 14–16/18 group. Non-vocational provision in particular has proved to be an educational success of recent years.

Higher Education   The most important development in higher education in the late nineteenth century, with far reaching effects into the twentieth, was the 1889 Universities Act. This brought to an end the traditional professor-student, master-pupil atmosphere, gave rise to a new staffing structure (readers, lecturers, etc), made new curricula possible (more flexible Ordinary degrees and a wider range of Honours subjects, and a move to applied science in BSc courses) and introduced new patterns of university administration (more power to the Court and the formation of a Secretariat). Courses were also opened to women. University extension evening classes expanded and in 1919 came under rationalised control (when the Report of the Committee on Adult Education recommended the formation of university extra-mural departments with provincial responsibility).

In the period after World War II vast changes were in store: (a) an explosion in demand for places arose from the great increase in the postwar birth rate; (b) new universities were created from existing institutions in Edinburgh, Glasgow and Dundee, and a completely new one in Stirling, on the recommendation in the Robbins Report on Higher Education in 1963; (c) the requirement of a group of Scottish Leaving Certificates as entrance qualification in the 1940s gave way to a flexible pattern, the 'certificate of attestation of fitness' being superseded in 1968 by more individual university entrance requirements; (d) state financial aid was increased in the 1950s and 1960s via the University Grants Committee and the Scottish Education Department; (e) a greater representation of non-professorial staff in administration and policy was achieved, via the Act of 1966.

One job the universities did not do for long was the training of teachers. In the early part of the post-1872 period, two-year courses were given in the church training colleges for non-graduates, but some scope was allowed for concurrent university classes for a few of these, a plan which for ten years at the turn of the century was operated by university-sponsored local committees, representing many educational interests. In 1906 a new Provincial Committee system marked the beginning of the state takeover of teacher training, and between 1913 and 1921 the four main colleges (at Moray House in Edinburgh, at Aberdeen, at Dundee and Jordanhill in Glasgow) crystallised out of former Church of Scotland/Free Church pairs. The organisation of teacher training received backing from a National Committee as from 1920, with separate colleges for Episcopal and Roman Catholic teachers, and this remained the pattern until 1958. In that year, Training Colleges became Colleges of Education with autonomous governing bodies. This, the present position, will be described later. Some points on twentieth-century Scottish teacher-education are listed below:

1. Every Scottish teacher, graduate or non-graduate, has been

required by law to train since 1906—a radically different position from that in England.

2. The Teacher's General Certificate for primary-school teaching could from 1906 be obtained either by two-year non-graduate (ie entirely in college) or one-year postgraduate (ie after university) training, the Special Certificate in one year by the University Honours graduate for higher secondary-school teaching; an endorsement (or extra certificate) for the earlier form of advanced elementary teaching by Ordinary (ie general three-year degree) graduates in one year, and the Technical Certificate in one post-diploma year by art, music, domestic science teachers and the like.

3. In 1906 the 'pupil teacher' became the 'junior student' who underwent from 15 to 18 a combined secondary and training course preparatory to the two-year college course; and in 1924 all forms of secondary 'pre-training' were replaced by training in a college. This was a significant moment in training history, and Scotland reached it ahead of many other nations.

4. In 1924 all male candidates for primary-school teaching were required to be graduates, a situation reversed only in the late 1960s.

5. Regulations of 1931 extended primary non-graduate women's training to three years.

6. Regulations of 1958, 1965 and 1967 took new 'College of Education' status (1958) and the formation in 1965 of a new professional 'General Teaching Council' into account. These were the main alterations after World War II, and 1969 amendments control the present situation.

At this point we may leave the beaten track of linear evolution and, in the next chapter, emerge on to the open plain of the contemporary scene in Scottish education.

C

2

Organisation, Administration and Finance

CENTRAL CONTROL

THE Scottish Education Department (SED) mentioned in the later stages of the foregoing historical account is one of four Departments forming the Scottish Office, which is based in St Andrew's House, Edinburgh. The others are devoted to Agriculture and Fisheries, Home and Health, and Development. There is a 'multi-purpose Minister', the Secretary of State for Scotland, at the head of the Scottish Office, but he is assisted in his duties by (a) a Minister of State and Parliamentary Under-Secretaries of State (the link with government and Parliament in London) and (b) Permanent and Assistant Permanent Under-Secretaries, who are the civil servants responsible for co-ordination of policy over the four Departments. At SED 'single Department level' a Secretary with his subordinate staff is in internal charge.

The Secretary of the SED is assisted by two Under-Secretaries of Department and nine Assistant Secretaries. The nine Assistant Secretaries run nine divisions of the Department, covering:

1. Primary and Secondary Education
2. Formal Further Education
3. Higher Further Education (including university matters)
4. Informal Further Education (also sport, recreation, arts)
5. Supply and Training of Teachers
6. Teachers' Service (eg salaries and superannuation)
7. Educational Building

34

8. Special Education etc
9. Finance, Planning and Statistics

But in addition, as a result of the Social Work (Scotland) Act, 1968, a Social Work Services Group with its own Under-Secretary and three Assistant Secretaries has been added to SED. Each of the Assistant Secretaries is responsible for a separate division in this group, covering respectively:

1. Social Work Reorganisation
2. Approved Schools, Remand Homes (delinquency), Adoption
3. Development of Local Authority Social Work Services

The Social Work Service Group, together with the local authorities and the voluntary organisations, can call on the advice of a Central Advisory Service under a Chief Advisor of Social Work, assisted by a Deputy and two Senior Advisors with territorial responsibility.

All the officials mentioned are responsible for major decisions on policy in their respective spheres of influence, while subordinate Branch heads see to the routine business of sectional areas within divisions.

The head of this administrative machinery is, of course, the Secretary of State himself. His relationship with Scottish education (and this is ultimately that of the government in London and of the Treasury for he is a member of the Cabinet) exists largely through the above SED organisation and decision structure, but not entirely so. In the sphere of finance, particularly, he operates through the Scottish Development Department and its general grants to local authorities, as well as directly through the SED and its specific grants to teacher training, grant-aided schools, central colleges of art, technology and the like.

The Secretary of State is also intimately concerned with the statutory aspect of Scottish education. (a) He is responsible for the issuing of Regulations dealing with all parts of the system or allied provision (eg regulations controlling teacher training courses, student grants, etc). Regulations are formulated in first draft, and an interval of six weeks is allowed for the statement of views by local authorities and others. After this they are redrafted on the basis of any modifications proposed, taken to Parliament, and come into force if approved, though they are subject for a further six weeks to scrutiny by members of Parliament who can still move their cancellation. Provisional regulations can be used if necessary to meet a special situation, but these have a limited life. (b) The Secretary of State also has the power to arbitrate in teacher-education authority clashes, if any such occur, over threatened dismissal from a post. His decision on the rights and wrongs of the case is final, but he cannot force the authority to reinstate the teacher. What he can do is to compel the payment of a year's salary (or as much as is necessary) to the dismissed teacher.

Through the SED also, the Secretary of State could be said to supervise the operation of *most* of the Scottish education system (the school system, its building and equipment, local proposals for comprehensive education, and so on). Health measures in school are not in the care of the SED, but supervised by the Home and Health Department; one other exception is the certification (now 'registration') of teachers, which has been transferred from the Secretary of State to the General Teaching Council, the profession's own 'self-control' body, and the first of its kind anywhere in the world.

Not all of the Department's work is done through such statutory instruments as Regulations or Codes (periodic statements on curricular or other internal matters). Circulars and memoranda are issued to announce state policy on some important theme, guide development or stimulate feedback of information. In 1965, for example, there appeared Circular 600 on the Reorganisation of Secondary Education on Comprehensive Lines, and also the Memorandum on Primary Education in Scotland, as good an expression of present trends in the primary school in Scotland as it is possible to find.

All the responsibilities of the SED are, in theory, therefore discharged by the Secretary of State. But in practice the work is done by the officials of the Department itself, in accordance with the policy for which the Secretary of State is ultimately answerable to Parliament. In summing up, one may say that, while local education authorities are certainly the responsible 'providers' of education, a strong central control is maintained on educational standards from Edinburgh. The situation is more like that in Scandinavia than that in England and Wales where there is such a diverse regional patchwork of education authorities.

Before passing from 'central' to 'local' organisation let us look at the work of an important arm of the SED, the Inspectorate (or 'Her Majesty's Inspectors of Schools'). Under HM Senior Chief Inspector, who is the chief decision- and policy-maker, there are at present seven Chief Inspectors, with either 'territorial' (east, west or Highland) or 'system' (primary, secondary, further education, teacher training) responsibility. There is, of course, some degree of overlap between these two kinds of function. But 'territorial' implies an overall concern with provision, planning and policy, while 'system' implies a curriculum development role.

Each Chief Inspector is assisted by a team of Inspectors in charge of subdivisional districts and junior colleagues. These subordinate staffs work in practice attached to divisions and districts. In addition, specialist inspectors are appointed for Special Schools, and for subjects such as music.

The function of the Inspectorate has traditionally been to keep a close eye on the schools and report back to the Department, but this relationship, sometimes a little tense in the past, is rapidly changing into one where the Inspector acts more and more as an adviser on curriculum matters and a co-worker with the educationists in the schools, the headmasters and their departmental heads. Thus the SED exerts a very real influence for progress in the schools of Scotland through the school visits of its Inspectors, and also through the increasing work-load of Inspectors on conferences, working-parties, national committees etc. If there is an area where innovation is needed (eg, audio-visual aids, moral education, educational research or secondary counselling and guidance) there is almost certain to be an Inspector already working in this field. Such influence usually has to be wielded in the local situation, where the actual provision of education takes place.

The following bodies also promote innovation and give advice:
General Teaching Council for Scotland (standards of, entry to,
registration in, and questions of possible dismissal from, the
teaching profession)
Scottish Certificate of Education Examination Board
Scottish Association for National Certificates and Diplomas
(SANCAD)
Council for National Academic Awards (CNAA)
City and Guilds of London Institute (CGLI)
Consultative Committee on the Curriculum
Various Councils for technical education, youth service, com-
mercial education, teachers' salaries, teachers' and local
government personnel associations and organisations. (Some
of these will be referred to in later chapters.)

LOCAL CONTROL

There are essentially two main elements in the structure of the
local education authority. The totally professional and permanent
Director of Education and his Assistant and/or Deputy Directors
are responsible for ensuring that the authority and its committee
are in the fullest possession of the best advice available on contemporary national education policy and its implications before
taking local decisions. They are also charged with the carrying
out of the resultant educational planning, and for controlling the
work of the schools. The Education Committee, partly elected,
partly appointed (by churches, teaching organisations and others
with educational expertise or special local vested interest),
does the actual decision-making. Those elected are members of
the county or town councils involved, and are in a majority;
appointed members, who on average constitute a quarter of the
committees, have in common expertise of some sort in the education of the area, or represent church interests or schools.

The function of the committee could be described as the control, supervision and provision of every facet of local education.
Ultimate decisions on finance, however, are a shared function of
the county council and the central government. The central
government makes its contribution (about 60 per cent) through

general grant from the Scottish Development Department (for all services including education) and specific grant to designated educational establishments from the Scottish Education Department.

The Education Committee's work is done through sub-committees, set up to deal with major problems (eg primary and secondary schools, or staffing) and through local area sub-committees representing a multiplicity of local outside interests. The present-day education authority's responsibilities include, in addition to education provision 'across the board', concern with every possible aspect of education within the county or city: the equipment of the school, its residential accommodation where necessary, informal outdoor and special education, guidance and all forms of welfare, and a host of minor tasks.

The early 1970s, however, have seen a new move to change the pattern of Scottish local government, and this, of course, will affect education. The Royal Commission on Local Government in Scotland, under the chairmanship of Lord Wheatley, proposed in its report of 1969 that the thirty-five existing local authorities, some of which are too small to bear efficiently the costs and tasks of administration (particularly the growing expenditure on education) should be replaced by seven large regions each with a minimum population of about 100,000. Within each of these regions the smaller administrative unit of the district would be the direct descendant of the old county, having approximately its size, but with boundaries redrawn to rationalise certain anomalies of the present system (eg Banchory in North Kincardineshire, which lies on a natural east-west communication line, is the educational centre for children living within easy reach on either side but in another county, Aberdeenshire, in both cases). Such new patterns would benefit school planning in the Highlands mainland area especially. The Commission also proposed that community councils should be set up to ensure the expression of local views.

The responsibility for education would reside with the large regions, under the aegis of a council with a large element of responsible, possibly salary-earning, councillors, and advised by

a powerful chief education officer. No educational power was
suggested (or at least not clearly) for the districts. It is on this
point that the Report has been most severely criticised, since it
would deprive the district of its present education officer and its
participation in educational provision. It is worthy of note that
some directors of education proved themselves educationists in
the highest sense by accepting the possibility that the best
interests of education might indeed be served by the larger unit,
despite the fact that this put the future of their own posts in
jeopardy. Two regions in particular were seen as problem areas:
(a) the proposed West Region, containing the Glasgow-centred
conurbation and half the population of Scotland (ie $2\frac{1}{2}$ million)
and (b) the proposed Highland Region, stretching from Shetland
to Kintyre and comprising half the Scottish land area. In the
former case, the huge population (seen as a unit for many purposes) seems impossibly large for the assessment and meeting of
local needs in schools; and in the latter, while wider planning for
a sparse population is inevitable, the separate island areas of
Orkney, Shetland and the Hebrides claim the right to detached
'special district' status because of their nature as self-contained,
sea-girt island chains. Whether the districts should continue to
be controlled by a subordinate education officer within the
region is open to question. If the districts are to be given some
form of partnership in the scheme, what are their powers to be?
Wheatley rejected as divisive the Scandinavian-type organisation
whereby education to sixteen (compulsory schooling) is run locally
at 'municipality' (district or old county) level, and post-compulsory schooling by the county region. Some critics of the Report
took the view that another kind of divided responsibility would
have been possible by allotting school provision to the district,
and reserving the more financially burdensome duties such as in-
service training, educational technology, audiovisual aids, and
educational planning to the region.

The protracted nature of the discussion, and the unexpected
change of government in mid-1970, together served to push the
findings of the Report into the background until January 1971,
when the first hint of impending government action was given by

articles of 4 and 5 January in *The Scotsman*. The main modifications to the Wheatley recommendations expected by the writer
of the articles were (a) separate organisation for relevant sections
of the Islands and the Borders and (b) increase in the number of
regional authorities over and above the seven already proposed.
Also, a strong plea was made for the giving of power to parish
councils at grass-roots level—an historical throwback to old
forms of Scottish administration.

In February 1971, the government published its White
Papers on the reform of local government in England and Wales
and in Scotland. The latter referred to the Wheatley Report of
1969 and the subsequent criticism and discussion of it by interested parties. As a 'prescription for action' (and not merely a
basis for discussion) its sets out clearly a structure of Scottish
local government and its implications for education in the late
70s and beyond. Instead of Wheatley's seven regions and thirty-
seven districts the pattern is now to be a modified structure of
eight regions and forty-nine districts (see map on p 42). The
main changes are in the reduction of the vast Highland Region by
the removal of part of Argyll and the Orkney/Shetland islands and
the creation of a new Border Region. Thus the West Region
becomes by far the greatest in population, having half of all Scots
in it (decentralisation will arguably be necessary here), and
Orkney and Shetland, for geographical reasons, retain a greater
measure of autonomy at district or second-tier level.

Most major local authority functions, including education, will
be handled at regional level. No control of education will be
retained by the district except in the case of Orkney and Shetland. Even there, education services of a specialist or costly
nature will be co-ordinated with those of the Highland Region.
The implication is that there is to be a new structure of chief
education officers, education councils etc, at regional level. The
financial arrangements for this were to be made clear by a Green
Paper to be published later.

The proposed timetable of change is that necessary legislation
will be put through in the Parliamentary session 1972–3, elections
will take place in 1974 and the new structure will operate from

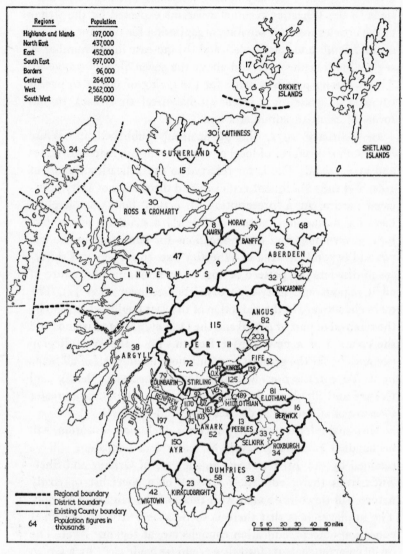

Regions	Population
Highlands and Islands	197,000
North East	437,000
East	452,000
South East	997,000
Borders	96,000
Central	264,000
West	2,562,000
South West	156,000

ORKNEY ISLANDS

SHETLAND ISLANDS

24

CAITHNESS 30

SUTHERLAND
15

6

ROSS & CROMARTY 30

9

NAIRN 8
MORAY 79
BANFF
ABERDEEN 52
68

INVERNESS 47
9
KINCARDINE 32
206

12

ANGUS 82
115

PERTH 203

ARGYLL 38
72
FIFE 52
KINROSS 138
CLK 145
DUNBARTON 79
STIRLING
KINCARDINE
125
RENFREW 201
92 107 9 109
MIDLOTHIAN
E.LOTHIAN 81
BERWICK 16
BUTE 170 163
103
75
LANARK 52
PEEBLES 13
SELKIRK 33
ROXBURGH 34
197
AYR 150
DUMFRIES 58
33
WIGTOWN 42
KIRKCUDBRIGHT 23

━━━ Regional boundary
─── District boundary
─·─· Existing County boundary
64 Population figures in thousands

0 5 10 20 30 40 50 miles

Regions and districts under proposed local government organisation in Scotland

1975, the whole process being one year later than in England and Wales.

FINANCE

There are two main sources of finance for education in Scotland, the central exchequer and the local authority rates (a small third source is the payment of fees in certain grant-aided or local authority schools). Exchequer payments are made, as has already been indicated, via general grants from the Scottish Development Department to a total of twelve services, including education, provided by local authorities. The Scottish Education Department itself also gives direct financial support to some institutions outside the school system such as colleges of education (this means that in Scotland these are virtually state colleges, whereas in England there is a pattern of church and local authority teacher training).

Apart from the general grant the education services receive money from four 'Department's votes', ie central expenditure for areas covered by Parliamentary finance: education, teachers' superannuation, social work and the Royal Scottish Museum in Edinburgh. Expenditure for session 1970–1 on education from this source was £32,600,000 in current and £4,600,000 in capital expenditure.

Total current expenditure by local authorities throughout Scotland in 1970–1 was £221,000,000 while central expenditure was about £32,500,000; the grand Scottish total, therefore, was in the region of £250,000,000—approximately one-tenth of the British national education expenditure, which is appropriate since the Scots constitute about one in ten of the national population. Estimated rates of growth for 1971–2 and 1972–3 were 5·1 per cent over the year 1969–70, these being planned for education within the context of the total national economy.

Some idea of the breakdown of cost of school education and cost per pupil is given in the chart overleaf, extracted from the HMSO Blue Book *Education in Scotland 1969*. Note that these figures are for the year 1968–9.

Costs of education authority schools and additional services
1968–9

	Total cost (all schools) £m.	Cost per pupil		
		All schools £	Primary schools and departments £	Secondary schools and departments £
Teachers' salaries .	71·9	77	52	129
School supplies and maintenance .	33·3	36	26	54
Loan charges (esti-mate). . .	17·3	19	11	34
TOTAL COST OF SCHOOLS	122·5	132	89	217
Additional services (net costs) Bursaries, board and lodging .	1·4	2		
Transport . .	3·0	3		
School health ser-vice . .	2·3	2		
Meals and milk .	10·3	11		
TOTAL COST OF ADDITIONAL SERVICES .	17·0	18		

A relatively new concept introduced by Circular 644 in 1967 is that of 'pooled expenditure', a system whereby local authorities take joint responsibility for a certain range of important allied educational services: further education, some (but not all) teachers' in-service courses, teaching of the hospitalised, training of educational psychologists, etc. Each local authority contributes to the pool on the basis of size, but is assisted with an appropriate amount from the central grant. This expenditure increased very quickly under the Labour government, but recently there has been some uncertainty about the future of the system and it is now restricted in financial scope by Circular 784 of 1971.

Central contribution was regulated by an Act of 1958,* and that of the local authorities by the 1962 Education Act. The latter has been simplified in structure by the Education (Scotland) Act of 1969, which has pared down archaic financial duties.

Some discussion has taken place in Scotland on the question of transferring more of the education bill to central government, particularly the increasingly heavy item of teachers' salaries. But general opinion at present favours the retention of the existing major (but not total) contribution of the central government. Objections that teachers might become civil servants and thus lose their freedom to choose employment are crucial in this argument.

From this brief account of educational finance in Scotland we go on to consider in some detail the contemporary educational system.

---

* Before 1958, 'percentage' grant implied 60 per cent help from the centre, specifically earmarked for education—an encouragement to a willing local authority to spend. Since 1958 'general grant' is fixed, on a population basis, as a sum for twelve services (including education, the largest item) provided locally. This, despite anxiety over possible local neglect of education, has in fact encouraged growth.

3

Pre-School and Primary Education

NURSERY SCHOOLS

IT should first be stressed, that the term 'pre-school' refers to education before the age of five, since in Britain compulsory primary schooling starts at that age.

Expanded state provision in this sector is unlikely for many years because of financial priorities. It is the opposite 'fringe' of compulsory education which is receiving attention first, in the form of extension of compulsory schooling from fifteen to sixteen. It may be that pre-school development will be next on the list for greater attention; even so, the Education Department in its mapping of trends does not foresee an increase in the numbers of children in the age range (2/3–4/5) within the school system (see table on pp 48–9).

Nevertheless, the Plowden Report of 1966 on primary education in England and Wales has been closely studied in Scotland, and its influence must be reckoned with. Plowden made strong recommendations for the expansion of nursery schooling, especially in deprived and disadvantaged urban areas. Certainly, Scotland has much less of this type of urban area than England and Wales, but where such problems exist they are equally as difficult.

By the Education (Scotland) Act of 1962, the local authority is *encouraged* to provide nursery schooling (a) if a number of parents ask for it, and (b) if sufficient numbers of children can be mustered in a suitable centre. This, needless to say, means that very little nursery education (in national terms) is actually provided. Relatively few education authorities take such initia-

46

tive, and they are mostly in the urban areas and in the central industrial belt. These, of course, are exactly the areas where most effort is needed.

Parallel with state nursery schooling, a certain amount of private provision is made, either in separate accommodation or attached to grant-aided or independent schools. It is difficult to estimate the size of the last group as there are no reliable statistics, but there are about 100 state- and grant-aided nursery schools at present, and about 50 attached classes. Numbers do, however, increase year by year, the main reason being (in the view of SED) the accommodation of two groups per day, and staff acceptance of this doubling of facilities. Older or unused primary school buildings are also being pressed into service.

An encouraging and significant development at the present time is the plan to use a new purpose-built school in Dunbartonshire (an example of a joint local authority-SED project) as a research centre for the study of nursery provision in a deprived area. Is this a side effect of Plowden or the result of Scottish initiative? In truth, it is something of both. In conjunction with research, some pre-service and in-service training of nursery teachers and nurses (the first group coming within the orbit of the colleges of education) is necessary also—and beginnings have been made with this by the Scottish Nursery Nurses Examination Board and by Fife, one of the most progressive of the Scottish local authorities.

In addition to this, the urban programme of the new Social Work Services Group of the Scottish Education Department has made £600,000 available in two stages to local authorities for the increase of nursery places. This invitation has been eagerly taken up by many areas in the form of proposals made every so often for various new forms of nursery schooling. Financial aid is also available for a variety of private play groups and similar bodies.

However, resources are limited and priorities have to be established, at least in the state-provided school. Criteria here tend to be deprivation or disadvantage in some form, physical or mental handicap for instance, or unstable home circumstances, or illness. An 'economic-political' criterion is also creeping in, in

Child population in pre-schooling (numbers, percentage and comparison with primary) 1960–88

	Age at 1 January	Actual									Forecast				
		1961	1962	1963	1964	1965	1966	1967	1968	1969	1970	1971	1972	1973	1974
Numbers in Thousands	Boys 2–4	3·7	3·2	3·2	3·3	3·5	3·7	3·9	4·3	5·2	5·9	5·9	5·9	5·9	6·0
	Boys 5–11	285·2	285·7	287·4	291·1	294·7	297·8	301·2	306·1	311·6	315·9	318·1	318·1	316·4	315·2
	Girls 2–4	3·5	3·2	3·2	3·1	3·4	3·6	3·7	4·1	5·1	5·6	5·6	5·6	5·6	5·7
	Girls 5–11	272·3	272·7	274·9	278·5	281·4	284·9	287·9	292·3	297·9	301·9	302·9	302·7	301·2	299·0
	Total 2–4	7·2	6·4	6·3	6·4	6·9	7·3	7·6	8·4	10·4	11·5	11·5	11·5	11·5	11·7
	Total 5–11	557·5	558·4	562·3	569·6	576·1	582·7	589·1	598·5	609·5	617·8	621·0	620·8	617·6	614·2
% of Age Group	Boys 2–4	2·6	2·2	2·2	2·3	2·4	2·5	2·6	2·9	3·6	4·1	4·2	4·3	4·4	4·6
	Boys 5–11	94·4	94·7	94·5	94·4	94·6	94·5	94·1	94·0	94·4	94·6	94·6	94·6	94·5	94·6
	Girls 2–4	2·6	2·3	2·3	2·2	2·4	2·6	2·6	2·9	3·7	4·2	4·2	4·3	4·4	4·6
	Girls 5–11	94·4	94·5	94·5	94·4	94·5	94·7	94·3	94·4	94·9	94·8	94·6	94·7	94·7	94·7
	Total 2–4	2·6	2·3	2·2	2·2	2·4	2·5	2·6	2·9	3·7	4·2	4·2	4·3	4·4	4·6
	Total 5–11	94·4	94·6	94·5	94·4	94·6	94·6	94·2	94·2	94·6	94·7	94·6	94·6	94·6	94·6

Forecast

	Age at 1 January	1975	1976	1977	1978	1979	1980	1981	1982	1983	1984	1985	1986	1987	1988
Numbers in Thousands	Boys 2–4	6·3	6·7	7·2	7·7	8·1	8·5	8·9	9·3	9·7	10·1	10·5	11·0	11·4	11·8
	Boys 5–11	309·8	304·5	298·3	294·7	294·5	294·9	296·5	300·0	305·0	310·5	314·9	318·3	321·0	323·5
	Girls 2–4	6·0	6·4	6·9	7·3	7·7	8·1	8·5	8·8	9·2	9·6	10·0	10·4	10·8	11·2
	Girls 5–11	294·2	289·0	282·9	279·3	279·0	279·8	281·1	285·1	289·9	294·8	299·1	302·4	304·8	307·3
	Total 2–4	12·3	13·1	14·1	15·0	15·8	16·6	17·4	18·1	18·9	19·7	20·5	21·4	22·2	23·0
	Total 5–11	604·0	593·5	581·2	574·0	573·5	574·7	577·6	585·1	594·9	605·3	614·0	620·7	625·8	630·8
% of Age Group	Boys 2–4	4·8	5·0	5·2	5·4	5·6	5·9	6·1	6·3	6·5	6·8	7·0	7·2	7·4	7·6
	Boys 5–11	94·6	94·6	94·5	94·5	94·5	94·4	94·5	94·4	94·4	94·5	94·5	94·5	94·5	94·5
	Girls 2–4	4·8	5·0	5·3	5·4	5·6	5·9	6·1	6·3	6·5	6·8	7·0	7·2	7·4	7·7
	Girls 5–11	94·7	94·8	94·7	94·6	94·5	94·6	94·5	94·6	94·6	94·6	94·6	94·6	94·6	94·6
	Total 2–4	4·8	5·0	5·2	5·4	5·6	5·9	6·1	6·3	6·5	6·8	7·0	7·2	7·4	7·6
	Total 5–11	94·7	94·7	94·6	94·6	94·5	94·5	94·5	94·5	94·5	94·5	94·5	94·5	94·5	94·5

Extracted from Table 2, *Scottish Education Statistics*, 1970.

that places are available for children of women teachers or intending teachers.

Private nursery schooling can be fairly described as confined to urban middle-class areas, and as selecting its pupils from families who can pay fees. A more deliberate form of selection in some groups is of children of good health, psychological adjustment and intelligence, a completely different segment of the population. A very large percentage of children, therefore, do not qualify for places in either state or private nurseries.

Internally, certain general truths tend to apply:

1. Size: state nurseries normally hold about 35–40 children, and private ones no more than about 27.
2. Age range: this is $2\frac{1}{2}$–5 years in state nurseries, and $3\frac{1}{2}$–5 in private nurseries.
3. Hours: state nurseries usually function all day, taking two groups consecutively; private usually take one group only, for half a day.
4. Staff: the state teacher probably has a certificate of training; the private teacher probably has not.

Nursery education itself is on the whole characterised by a very progressive educational philosophy and practice. The child's environment is usually attractive, colourful and equipped to meet every conceivable need. The nursery school is often a 'small child's world' created out of scaled-down furniture and toilet facilities, with plenty of storage for toys and other objects. Space is very carefully regulated by the SED as to minimum standards with an eye to child health, and the children have the benefit of the ordinary school welfare and medical services. A careful control is maintained over diet and regular rest.

The activities of nursery school are on the whole play-based and widely varied, so that the child can express himself, build, make things, climb, and develop socially and psychologically through the media provided, eg sand, toys, art materials, nature tables, and so on.

It is generally agreed among educationalists in Scotland that the nursery school has proved its worth, and that any expansion of these services would therefore be most valuable, especially in the context of increasing urbanisation with its 'high-rise' living and consequent family stresses. It is a truth easily observable in Scottish education as a whole, that progressive influences start at the foot of the age scale and work upwards. We shall see this in the following account of the primary school.

PRIMARY SCHOOLS

It is in the sector of primary education that we find the first indication that there is no such thing as a 'British education system' (although overseas readers are almost certain to gain this impression from books and articles by English educationists— most of whom hardly acknowledge the existence of a separate school tradition and pattern in the north of the United Kingdom). Scottish primary education lasts for seven years from the age of five to the age of twelve; not as in England from five to eleven. The term 'eleven-plus' as a description of the selective primary-secondary transfer machinery of the period before the 1965–6 comprehensive schooling initiative was, strictly speaking, incorrect in Scotland.

Here 'transfer' or 'qualifying' described the procedure officially, and it was in fact 'twelve-plus'. At the time of writing it seems highly likely that in most parts of Scotland the model of seven years primary and six secondary will be retained in view of the almost universal choice by Scottish local authorities (unlike the English LEAs with six possible education system patterns) of the so called 'orthodox' all-through (ie for six years in one place) secondary school beginning at the age of twelve. One county, Stirlingshire, has deviated from this norm by proposing to experiment from 1972–3 in the Grangemouth area with the 'middle school' which in Scotland would mean a school containing children of ten to fourteen, or Primary 6 to Secondary 2, which implies a 5–10, 10–14, 14–18 structure. This is an idea of tremendous promise, advocated strongly by some Scottish educationists for the Highland counties as a form of 'decentralised centralisation' (to translate an expressive Norwegian phrase) designed to meet needs of children, transport problems, economic provision and so on. But no decision has been taken in this direction, and it is the writer's view that such solutions may become practical politics in Highland education only after regional reform of local government has been made a reality. Edinburgh also proposed to use middle schools, but secondary teachers there opposed what they considered to be a Machiavellian political move to 'dilute' secondary standards and to infiltrate primary teachers into the secondary sphere. The general Scottish structure at the moment remains based on a 5–12 primary education.

A further refinement of structure is that within the seven grades of the primary school (normally styled Primary 1 to 7), the first two (Primary 1 and 2) are looked upon as the 'infant' stage, and are very much a continuance of the philosophy and practice outlined above for nursery schools. This is in a way an implicit recognition that, although part of compulsory schooling, they are in fact kindergarten and their purpose is to encourage adjustment to social living through play and self-expression. This is further underlined by the fact that in very many primary schools a teacher with Froebel training (the Froebel Certificate needs a fourth year in College of Education after the completion of the three-year Primary Diploma) or at least an infant-teaching qualification, is in charge of this stage, under the general direction of the head teacher. Primary 3–7 is primary schooling in the fully accepted sense of the phrase catering for the seven- to twelve-year-olds in reading, number and environmental studies.

There have been since the war two major national reports on primary education in 1950 and 1965–6. Between them, though much maligned in many quarters, they have gone a long way to give a 'policy momentum' to the modern primary with its integrated curriculum, group methods etc, as we know it now. There are solid indications that in the early 1970s primary teachers are on the whole moving with the progressive spirit of the report of 1965–6. What has stimulated change is the increasing teamwork between head teachers (who are influential figures in the Scottish school system), the relatively new county primary advisers (whose function is to promote modern primary schooling within the context of national policy but in close touch with local needs), college of education lecturers, the staff of the Inspectorate, and of course, the teachers who are creating everywhere a much more meaningful learning environment in the classroom. There is an exciting sense of liberation in the Scottish primary, and great future promise.

It goes without saying that the primary schools are wholly compulsory and parents have a duty to provide for the education of their children within state or other schools. The great majority of Scottish children attend local authority primary schools, normally in a specified zone of the local education area. Parental wishes are in theory taken into account, but the avoidance of excessive expenditure in transport and the acceptance by most parents of the zone school tend to place most children close to home. This has obvious implications of a sociological kind, in that there are 'good' and there are 'bad' schools. It is with the latter that the 1950 and 1965/6 reports, the urban development programmes and the Scottish Education Department are acutely concerned in a system aiming at equality of opportunity.

The school year in Scotland (affecting secondaries also) lasts generally from late August until the end of June or beginning of July, and must have '400 attendances' (ie 200 days) in any year, an attendance referring to either a morning or afternoon session. The latest trend, however, is towards the use of a four-term year, since the August to Christmas term is generally agreed to be too long for young children. This new pattern will allow a break in late October. It is by no means a new idea, since the 'tattie' holidays (for potato harvesting or other agricultural work) are an old tradition. But modern urban conditions have strangely enough created again a need for this arrangement.

Scottish primary schools have not, for the most part, used the system of streaming, or class organisation based on levels of ability, so common in England. This is, of course, because of the largely rural and very democratic character of Scottish parish schooling. The term 'two stream' used of a few larger urban Scottish primaries, is misleading. In Scotland it means two parallel and 'similar mixed ability profile' classes on one age level. Having said that, however, it is necessary to state that in

some larger urban primaries, especially in the cities, and above all
in Edinburgh, the streaming pattern on the English model has
been found in many schools.

Other forms of experimental class structure have come into
use in some areas, such as 'family grouping' (classes consisting of
an age spread over two to three years especially in the infant
stage), in order to allow for better social development while still
providing the normal range of educational activities. As yet,
there is no cause to think that this will be adopted widely. Between Primary 5 and 7 (ages ten to twelve) the whole of this
'senior' age range can be regrouped according to special interests
and aptitudes to give them something of the specialist care that
the secondary school has traditionally offered in the past. Thus
choice is increased, motivation of teacher and pupil increases, and
there is some reason for questioning whether the normal 'one
teacher one class' system is still the best at this stage. In fact,
one can see a 'middle school philosophy' developing here, even if
there is yet no officially separated middle school or middle stage.
The same trend can be seen in those areas where there is a great
deal of co-operation between the staffs of the secondary school
and of the upper stages of the local primary. It could be said that
the old tradition of the all-age school, the combined primary and
secondary in larger rural centres, is influencing modern reform.
There is some possibility that the teacher-training system may
have to take more account of this 'middle area' of schooling than
is possible at present. As long as the school system is officially
divided by a physical and curricular break into 'twelve-minus'
and 'twelve-plus' it is impossible to do other than channel
student teachers along two separate routes to the Primary and
Secondary Qualifications. If a middle stage were to be recognised
officially—even if only in some regions—then the colleges would
naturally have to provide appropriate training.

Post-war trends   By the end of World War II the content
of the primary curriculum had already expanded vastly from the
traditional nineteenth-century 'three Rs' to include some of the
aesthetic, physical and oral emphases familiar today—and this
expansion has certainly continued since the war. This is due

largely to intensified discussion on the aims and objectives of the primary—or 'basic'—school in our modern society, and also to postponed selection and democratisation of opportunity.

Nevertheless, it is true that despite social pressures and educational policies the acceptance of curricular change by teachers has been slow and typically 'canny' (the Scots word means cautiously and calculatingly conservative). Certainly in the 1940s and 1950s Scottish Education Department initiatives to widen the curriculum content and to encourage emphasis on oral work tended to be thought of as ivory-tower idealism, remote from classroom realities. But the changes suggested have in fact come slowly: there is much more emphasis now on children learning and discovering for themselves; children are being encouraged by every means to express themselves in spoken as well as written language; discovery mathematics and junior science figure prominently in the curriculum, and French has been introduced (but this has been less successful from lack of qualified teachers—perhaps another argument for access to primary by secondary specialists in a middle school). Subject integration is now becoming the rule rather than the exception, so that the class day moves from topic to topic rather than from period to period—and generally the children work in informal separate groups, not in regular serried ranks as in the past. The Report *Primary Education in Scotland* (1965–6) already mentioned, emphasised subject integration and encouraged the creation of the Scottish primaries of the 1970s where no area of life is untouched by pupil discovery, where an increasing number of formerly secondary school skills are reaching the senior levels, and where pupils, flexibly organised, investigate areas of knowledge in a three-dimensional way. All this is happening in Scotland some years later than in England. The academic tradition affecting primary school has died hard.

The position of the teachers is very free in the sense that although individual class teachers may plan their day on the lines suggested in the 1965–6 Report there is a high degree of flexibility as to what takes place in the classroom between 9am and 3.30/4pm, and in what order, and teachers are able as a result to follow up any promising unexpected lines of class interest.

In this educational climate are the three Rs neglected? Rather it would be true to say that an effort is being made to organise learning ever more effectively in this area. In reading, the basic method tends to be a combination of the phonic and the 'look-and-say', remedial attention for the backward is much more in evidence, and aids such as flash cards and reading laboratories are employed. The use of the Initial Teaching Alphabet, designed to phoneticise and simplify the spelling of English, has been experimented with but still arouses much controversy. In number learning there is much more emphasis on the formation of number concepts and understanding, but it must be admitted that some teachers feel a loss of accuracy results from the abandonment of the old-style drill in number. Some schools take part in nationally initiated primary mathematics projects, and much attention was focused on decimalisation, followed now by metrication of weights and measures. Writing is still regarded as an important skill, but the older aesthetically beautiful styles have given way to various quick and easy to use forms of joined script or italic writing. Legibility is probably the only remaining link between old and new.

Interesting experiments are being carried out in the fields of primary drama, music, poetry and physical education, and, in certain schools, in integrated combinations of all of these. Audio-visual aids—the tape recorder, the film projector, radio and television programmes for schools as disseminated by the national and local networks—are being increasingly and intelligently used.

No account of contemporary Scottish primary schooling would be complete without mention of the increasing use of imaginative projects designed around some compelling theme such as space exploration, the local community, or the environment of another school. These have been set up with much success both by individual teachers and their classes and by sub-areas within local authorities. Particularly successful has been the Springburn project in Glasgow, which was concerned with the study of the local environment, and aimed to give pupils a wide and integrated learning experience, and to act as a model to Scottish teachers of a school run on the lines of the 1965–6 Report. The local authority's primary advisers, the staff of Jordanhill College of Education and teachers all co-operated in the planning of the project. Eventually a film record will make it widely available and will be used to supplement the programme of concurrent in-service training for teachers which ran parallel with the scheme.

Assessment of pupils in the modern primary school depends upon a combination of standardised achievement, diagnostic, attainment and intelligence tests at different levels and for different purposes, together with the teacher's own periodic tests. This heavy load of assessment is another legacy of the old Scottish primary tradition with its now much criticised insistence on competition, class places and all the paraphernalia of an age in which the supreme goal was to squeeze through the bottleneck of the academic secondary. The removal of this bottleneck by the abolition of twelve-plus selection is a major reason why the Scottish primary curriculum has changed.

Impetus is being given to the whole process of change by local authority primary advisers and by the setting up of teachers' centres in many authorities' areas. The function of the advisers—who are amongst the most influential newcomers to the Scottish educational scene in recent years—is to promote within their areas of responsibility a primary schooling that is modern in every sense, and in line with national policy. This is especially important in the Highland and rural counties, where the inevitable physical and professional isolation of the teacher has in the past been one of the main obstacles to a curriculum providing the rural child with a fare as rich as that of his urban peer. The adviser is not, of course, tied to fulfilling these goals in any one way, but tends to be involved in local in-service courses and work of teachers' centres, and serves on national conferences on education. It is in the teachers' centres, perhaps, that the adviser tends to work most in conjunction with college of education lecturers on curriculum development. These centres have proved invaluable for providing teachers with opportunities to discuss professional matters—at conferences, on courses, on panels, for instance. No longer is it the case that teachers only discuss their objectives when they are summoned to a meeting by the director of education and subjected to an agenda.

In-service courses for primary staff have increased rapidly in all areas, on all aspects of the curriculum, and are held by colleges of education and by local authorities both in summer vacation and in term time. Worthy of special mention, perhaps, are the courses dealing with primary mathematics, which have attracted large numbers of teachers (and which are having most productive effects in the schools) and the 'simulated-situation' type of course for actual and potential primary head teachers. It is possible that in future such in-service training as this may be a prerequisite for promotion with, of course, salary incentives attached, and that attendance at other courses may also lead to posts of special responsibility within primary schooling.

The parents, as the 'adult representatives' of the consumers of education, also have to be taken into account. Contacts between school and home vary in their adequacy, quality and effectiveness according to the social background. There are instances of good parent-teacher associations, parents-only associations which constitute a local pressure group unfortunately without school connection, and also of difficult urban situations where parents with a 'folk memory' of school as a formidable place have to be weaned from their dislike of meeting teachers. Less formal, rather different, contacts are made at Open Days, Parents' Days and Education Weeks, which are becoming more frequent.

Much thought is currently given, again under the impetus of the Primary Report of 1965-6, to what might be called the deployment and organisational functions of staff. The objectives suggested here for the headmaster envisage his job as concerned with every aspect of school policy, staffing, pupils' attainment, welfare, physical environment and co-ordination of teaching and ancillary staff effort. His is a roving commission, to familiarise himself with conditions and problems in every class, to give him time for teaching and close contact with his children, to render him fully informed in his relationships with parents, and to pass on full information on his pupils to the secondary school. The class teacher is seen as an adaptable, imaginative planner, but not

necessarily as omnicompetent. The head must know his staff's
varying abilities and use them as far as they exist, phasing in the
specialist help of visiting teachers at suitable times and places.
In other words the primary school is coming to be regarded in a
sociological light as an organised enterprise with a need for
skilled leadership at top and middle levels.

In the rural areas many small schools have been closed down
and education has been centralised, partly because of depopulation, partly to make economic use of buildings and staff, and
partly to enrich the curriculum. Here again the possible rele-
vance of the middle school is seen. Nevertheless, although this
trend goes on apace, there are still very many small one or two-
teacher schools in the remoter rural areas.

In the field of research, there is at present much reason for
encouragement. Work is co-ordinated for the most part by the
Scottish Council for Research in Education in Edinburgh, and
participators in it are the universities, colleges of education and
local authorities. Teachers are not yet in the van of such work
but will probably play an increasing part. The whole tone of the
Primary Report encourages experimentation.

Lastly, we come to the question of transfer to secondary
education. In 1946 the term 'secondary' was applied to all forms
of twelve-plus education, but from this stemmed the procedure
of selection by a battery of tests for entry to the senior secondary
or academic school. This was gradually phased out so that the
term 'transfer' came to be used rather than 'selection'. Each
local authority has had to submit a suitable scheme to be
approved by the Secretary of State for primary-secondary
transfer. Usually these transfer schemes have relied on verbal
reasoning and attainment tests, teachers' estimates, and objective English and arithmetic tests. This facilitated allocation to
certificate or non-certificate (ie academic or non-academic)
courses in secondary schools. The procedure is administered by
a Transfer Board in each area, against whose decision the parent
can appeal—to the Secretary of State if necessary. But the parent
does not have the right to decide the pupil's course contrary to
education authority advice. Most appeals have in the past been

dismissed and the Board's decision upheld. However, the Departmental Circular 614 of 1966 has encouraged a move to a possible two-year period of orientation (the 'common course') in secondary schools, thus postponing selection decisions. Probably the likeliest development in the future is greater co-operation than now exists between primary and secondary staffs in the middle years of schooling. In any case the dovetailing of primary and secondary education has already begun and is likely to continue.

4
Secondary Education

THE most useful introduction to the current situation in Scottish secondary schooling seems to be an account of those factors (reports, memoranda, circulars, examination developments and the like) which have stimulated growth in this sector since World War II. But let us remember that the context within which all developments have taken place is a six-year school, for children aged twelve to eighteen. In other words, a full secondary education makes it possible for any willing pupil to stay in school to the age of eighteen. Having said that, however, one must also point out that the upper age-limit of compulsory schooling is sixteen, having only recently been raised from fifteen where it has stayed since the 1940s.

A SURVEY OF RECENT DEVELOPMENTS

The 1945 Act, as the earlier historical account (p 29) indicated, specified that all twelve-plus education should be regarded as secondary, and created the bipartite system of five- or six-year senior secondary and three-year junior secondary schools. The former were to provide courses leading to Higher Leaving Certificate and Sixth Year (one year, 17–18, in Scotland); the latter were to terminate in the county Junior Leaving Certificate. A common practice in the sixth year of senior secondaries at this time was to prepare for the bursary competition of universities (a form of scholarship examination).

In 1950 a new decision was taken on the form of the Higher Leaving Certificate entry qualification for university. Instead of a 'group pass', much more flexibility was to be allowed in the number and type of Higher passes.

61

In 1955 a Scottish Education Department Blue Book *Junior Secondary Education* was published. This emphasised the necessity of education for all-round development, leisure and work, and stressed the importance of the school environment. Although this has been widely regarded as a definitive and worthwhile statement on the purpose of the non-academic secondary school, it failed to achieve for it the hoped for equal status with the senior secondary.

In 1959 the main instrument for change was the publication of the *Report of the Working Party on the Curriculum of the Senior Secondary School*. This recommended the introduction of the Ordinary ('O') Grade Certificate (at age 16) and concerned itself with the effectiveness of the fifth and sixth years (16–18) of secondary education.

This was followed in 1960 by the report of an Advisory Council Special Committee, *Post-Fourth Year Examination Structure in Scotland*. This recommended the retention of the Scottish Higher in fifth year (age 17) as an objective indication of pupil attainment, and a useful tool for university entrance— but went further to concern itself with the provision of a purposeful and directed sixth year (17–18), recommending (as previously in 1947) the introduction of an English-style Advanced Grade of the Scottish Leaving Certificate. Taking Scottish conditions into consideration, however, it was stressed that the A Grade should not be a compulsory curriculum development, in view of the smallness of some rural secondaries and the probable lack of staffing for such courses. Thus in 1959–60 there emerged examinations at 16, 17 and 18—a situation reflected in the late 1960s and early 1970s in England in the proposals for a Q (qualifying grade, at 17) and F (further grade, at 18) to follow the existing O level. However, the A proposal came to nothing, after adverse criticism of specimen papers in 1964. In that year the sixth-year question was taken a step further, but this will be dealt with on p 64.

These years of growing disquiet are reflected to some extent in the replacement, in 1962, of the Lower Leaving Certificate at age 17 in a range of subjects (a certificate available only in the

senior secondary) by the O Grade Certificate at 16. The importance of this change was that the examination could be taken
either in the existing senior secondary or in any junior secondaries which cared to 'grow' a 15–16 year beyond legal leaving
age (fourth year in Scotland, fifth in England). This was an
import from the English system, and has proved to be one of the
most beneficial in Scottish educational history, in that since its
inception a fast-increasing percentage of Scottish fifteen-year-
olds have decided to stay on at school, drawn by the new incentive. At present almost half of these are attempting O Grade.
What this meant for the secondary education of the 60s in Scotland was that the clearcut bipartite system disappeared and many
secondaries in fact became four-year (12–16) schools. This has
done much to make transition to comprehensive unification at
secondary level easy—since many Scottish local authorities use
a linked system of four- and six-year secondaries in their comprehensive educational planning.

Also in this year, the administration of the external examination system was handed by the Scottish Education Department
to the newly created Scottish Certificate of Education Examination Board, so that the O and H examinations became officially
described as SCE Ordinary and Higher.

The year 1963 was significant for the publication of the now
famous Brunton Report (named after the then Senior Chief
Inspector of Schools). The philosophy of this Report has been
summed up many times in the phrases 'vocational impulse' and
'work-based courses'. In other words the Report gave impetus in
the 1960s to the provision of a range of courses for the less
academically inclined teenager, on the assumption that learning
geared to future employment in a known local job situation would
be meaningful and motivating. Criticisms have been heard since
that this is simply disguised bipartitism at a later stage, that it
encourages the enslavement of youngsters to a narrow vocational
treadmill, and so on. But some Scottish areas, at least, have as a
result provided a large 'package' of job-oriented options in their
schools. One area of discussion opened up by such courses has
been the possibility of providing 'bridging courses' for those

needing something in between an entirely O Grade course and one devoid of O Grades.

The general election in 1964 gave the country a Socialist instead of a Conservative government, and 1965–70 (until the Conservative return in 1970) was a period of central government pressure towards a comprehensive school system. This pressure was initiated in Scotland by Government Circular 600 of 1965— the counterpart of the Department of Education and Science Circular in England and Wales 10/65*—requiring local authorities to formulate plans for comprehensive schooling and submit them for approval within a specified time. Circular 600 recommended that the orthodox form of secondary education should be the continuous six-year (12–18) school. This was in striking contrast to 10/65 which, drawing on local authority experimentation, suggested no fewer than six forms of acceptably flexible comprehensive structure. The result of the Scottish circular has therefore been—with the notable exception of Stirlingshire's three-tier planning for one part of the county—that Scottish local authorities have opted for the one-tier (12–18) secondary school, in some cases with associated four-year (12–16) schools intended either as eventual full secondaries, or as sub-area feeders for the central six-year school. This, in the view of some in Scottish education, is unfortunate since some parts of Scotland would in fact greatly benefit from flexible school structures such as are found in England and Wales. Fuller discussions of the patterns adopted will be entered into later in this chapter.

In 1966 the Scottish Certificate of Education Examination Board produced its solution to the sixth-year problem (see p 62). This was announced in the Board's Circular 2 as the new Certificate of Sixth Year Studies, to be available in schools from 1968, in seven subjects (English, French, Physics, Geography, Art, Economics and Secretarial Science). Since then it has made an annual appearance: in 1968 with the above seven subjects, and in subsequent years adding Chemistry, German, History,

---

* These circulars, while not having the force of law, indicate periodically detailed government educational policy. Series run separately for English and Scottish systems.

Latin, Mathematics and Gaelic. This examination does not have precisely the same status as the English A Grade in that it is only recognised as a University entrance qualification in a small number of English universities at present and not officially in Scotland at all. But it has indeed given, so say the Scottish schools, impetus and direction to sixth-year pupils. In view of its year-by-year expansion and the likelihood of its covering the whole subject range before the 1970s are far spent, the British universities may one day feel constrained to recognise its validity, and then it would have to be put on the same footing as the English A Grade for university entrance on both sides of the 'tartan curtain'. The reluctance of existing universities to increase the range of qualifications acceptable for entry may be due to the increasing numbers of qualified applicants for too few places.

The most useful information available on the evolution of the secondary school via development of examinations and/or curriculum comes from Circular 3 (1970) of the SCE Examination Board. This is, in effect, a transcript of two very important addresses to a nationally representative conference of Scottish education personnel in Moray House College of Education, Edinburgh, in March of that year. These addresses, coupled with the recorded discussion of concurring and conflicting viewpoints, are a good example of the way in which 'the centre' in Scottish education maintains a healthy consultation with all interests in the system.

Main issues of the immediate future are dealt with. First, what is to be done about the O Grade examination now that compulsory schooling is extended to sixteen? What incentive to completion of education can be offered to those below the top 30 per cent of ability for whom the O Grade was originally designed? Should the 'O' be extended in a new form to those in the average levels—or a national 'Scottish Certificate of Secondary Education' be created on the pattern of the existing English CSE? Since Scottish academic traditions die hard, it is difficult to forecast the settlement of this. The second issue concerns the structure and effect of the examination pattern at sixteen-plus, and the need

E

for it to serve the pupil better than hitherto in encouraging independent habits of study, and preparing him for higher education
entry. In this area of the sixteen-to-eighteen population, where
expansion will take place rapidly, as in all advanced countries in
the 1970s, little has been done to prepare for it. Educational
thinking has been concerned with the lower secondary ranges and
has done no more than nibble at the massive question of developing the whole of upper secondary schooling to meet the demands
of swelling numbers.

This inevitably will be discussed in the second half of the
1970s in Scotland, when lower secondary comprehensive schooling has been properly established and the twelve-to-sixteen
problem dealt with.

In 1970 there was a determined attempt to come to terms with
the private sector of secondary schooling, and to establish its
relationship with, and participation in, current state policy in
secondary education. This was embodied in the *Second Report of
the Public Schools Commission* (for the mystified non-British
reader, 'Public' schools are private, fee-paying educational
establishments of some prestige). Volume III of the Report
dealt separately with the Scottish system and situation. (More
will be said about this later; see pp 85–93). It was, of course, the
result of years of work initiated by a Socialist government and
completed only just within their term of office. The objective
was to estimate the future function of the private sector in some
kind of co-ordinated partnership with a state policy that aimed
at reducing social division of the kind often said to be fostered by
private schooling. It is fascinating to speculate on what use a
Conservative government will be able to make of the Scottish
report's findings. Certainly there is little likelihood that it will
prove eager for the kind of public-private integration suggested,
but there may yet be pressure in several educational quarters for
its reconsideration as a 'blue-print'. The approach of a general
election will perhaps have an effect here.

After this swift reconnaissance of the recent development of
the secondary sector, it is necessary to consider in a little more
detail what may be termed 'major areas' in contemporary

Scottish secondary schooling. The first of these is the policy of change from selective to comprehensive schooling.

COMPREHENSIVE POLICY

The Scottish Education Department classifies state secondary schools under three headings:

1. Selective (offering either five-year Higher courses or non-certificate only)—this is a decreasing category, including as it does former senior and junior secondaries. To expect it to disappear completely would probably be optimistic, in view of the problems of unification in, for example, the island areas of the north and north-west.

2. Comprehensive (offering both non-academic and academic courses; based on an initial common course orientation/guidance phase of one to two years and unselective in its intake from feeder primaries).

3. Part-selective, part-comprehensive (offering various combinations of non-certificate and certificate options based on the common course and in six- or four-year secondaries).

Obviously the only generalisation one can make is that more and more schools are becoming comprehensive as the years progress. The figures for 1968–9, for instance, show that about 60 per cent of twelve-year-olds entered schools with an unselected, mixed-ability intake in that school session. There was an expected increase over the three years to 1972 in view of a five-year building programme for new schools from 1967 to 1972. The Education Act of 1969 (not mentioned in the historical survey) introduced the new concept of 'school education' in removing the references to separate categories of 'primary and secondary' and easing all forms of school-to-school transfer. Further controversial legislation planned for 1971 would have compelled local authorities to 'go comprehensive'. But the change to a Conservative government has removed this possibility for the time being.

In Edinburgh and Glasgow, part of the pattern for many years has been the somewhat curious phenomenon of feepaying state schools; these are academic secondaries with centuries of

tradition behind them, competing for prestige in learning and
sport with the grant-aided schools—especially in Edinburgh,
where only a native could possibly understand the complexities
of status accorded to the various types of secondary school! These
schools were required to relinquish feepaying by the 1969 Act,
and indeed Edinburgh in particular promised to be a classic test
case of conflict between the national comprehensive education
policy and the determination of a Conservative local education
committee (supported by vociferous parental groups interested
in the feepaying schools) to maintain an influential selective
sector within their area. But local decision to bow to national
policy as from session 1970–1 effectively postponed the 'crunch'
until after the general election so that the Socialist government's
requirement in fact has not had to be met because of the change
of government. So Edinburgh maintains a *status quo* though now
with a narrow Socialist majority. Nevertheless, it is a fact that
comprehensive schooling continues to appear throughout the
county, since it is by no means unsupported by the present
government.

As far as the general pattern of comprehensive provision is
concerned, a certain amount has been said here and there already,
but an extract from information prepared for the writer by the
Scottish Education Department will serve to sketch in the general
national picture. This extract is dated 1969, so that two points
must be remembered: (a) on the whole, despite the change of
government, local authorities are still very much committed to
this programme, but there is now no element of compulsion or
insistence on any degree of uniformity; (b) the three-tier 'middle
school' plan is now confined to Stirlingshire only (see also pp
80–1).

> Scottish authorities favour the 'all through' comprehensive
> school extending over six years and providing a full range of
> secondary courses for all pupils from a particular area. This form
> of organisation is common in plans for urban areas and centres of
> population in rural areas. Where population is relatively scattered
> provision is necessarily centralised in comparatively few six-year
> schools. In outlying areas a number of four-year 'junior high
> schools' are proposed, which are comprehensive for classes S.I

and S.II, transfer potential Higher grade pupils to the central
six-year schools at the end of class S.II and themselves provide
non-certificate and SCE Ordinary grade courses in classes S.III
and S.IV. While four- and six-year schools are associated mainly
in rural areas, such an arrangement will be necessary in a number
of urban areas until the ultimate schemes of 'all through' schools
can be developed. In a few such areas 'two tier' organisations
have been or are about to be introduced as an alternative to long
delay in building up a system of 'all through' schools: these
organisations comprise junior high schools feeding potential
Higher grade pupils at the end of class S.II into 'senior high
schools', which cater for only certificate pupils from classes S.III
to S.VI. This form of organisation is, however, normally regarded
as a step towards an ultimate pattern of six-year schools. A further type of organisation which is planned is the 'three tier
system' which embraces lower schools (classes P.I to P.V),
middle schools (classes P.VI to S.II) and upper schools from
S.III to S.VI. Transfer between each stage is on a fully comprehensive basis. The approved schemes of two education authorities—Edinburgh and Stirlingshire—feature such an organisation
for parts of their areas, and it is expected to come into operation in
the early 1970s. In certain areas of scattered population small
junior secondary schools are to continue meantime, for geographical and social reasons anticipated by Circular No 600, but
authorities have been asked to keep the future of such schools
under close review.

We now turn to the internal organisation in the secondary
school at its various curricular levels, and in important curricular
areas, resulting from the above 'external' comprehensive policy.

THE FIRST TWO YEARS (12–14)

While it is impossible to say categorically that these two years
have a fixed national form in every detail (as they do have, in the
approximately corresponding grades of the Swedish school, for
instance) officially these are the years of the 'common course' or,
in international educational language, the 'orientation phase'.
This certainly is the part of secondary school curriculum which
currently causes most discussion, experimentation, variation,
controversy and soul searching. Since the Scottish headmaster is
an individual of much power and influence, what happens in each

school depends at the moment very much on the extent of his concurrence with the official policy on the early secondary years. Having said that, however, one must also add that there is an inexorable growth of feeling that the entry to secondary of the primary school intakes must be an unselected one. Therefore it is becoming gradually truer that the intake to a secondary school in the first year is allocated to classes of an all-ability range, based either on a random alphabetic grouping, or else organised in several parallel 'similar profiles' containing the whole IQ range from high to low ability.

It is rapidly becoming general for information of every relevant kind to be supplied from the feeder primaries to the neighbourhood secondary about each pupil, so that the secondary head can use it in his decisions on the pupil's future. At this crucial changeover stage, also, there is increasing local (and indeed individual) initiative in forming ties between the primary and the secondary school. This takes the form of visits by staffs of each institution to the other (mostly, so far, by secondary teachers to the primary), visits by primary pupils to the secondary, some 'cross-teaching', a few highly organised and commendable attempts by groups of headmasters to work in committee, and so on. Parents are also being consulted more than before.

While the mixed ability trend dominates, there are also variations upon it. Some schools put the whole cohort of twelve-year-olds into a total spread of ability. Others have a 'head, body and tail' arrangement with an 'a' class, several widely spread classes and a remedial class; while yet others have a two-tier plan dividing the 100-plus IQ range into classes, and the 100-minus range similarly. One could go into further detail, but this will suffice to show the range of experimentation which goes on—or perhaps the degree of headmasters' belief in the principle of comprehensive education.

A fundamental difference between the Scottish secondary school and the English is that, even before comprehensive policy, a much larger slice of the age group entered the academic secondary in Scotland. Only the urban areas resembled the English pattern in touching about 20 per cent, while in the rural areas—of which Scotland is largely composed and where Scottish tradition in education has always been purest—the level entering certificate pre-Higher education courses was more typically about 35 per cent. The description 'entering certificate courses' is more strictly accurate of the rural secondary, since to a considerable extent the rural secondary or 'omnibus' school has contained not only senior secondary, but local junior secondary pupils. To this extent the rural secondary has always been to some extent comprehensive, though not internally. Therefore the move to a national comprehensive pattern affecting the external system and the internal organisation of the school also has been more natural and less painful by far than in England.

When allocated, then, what is this 'common course' that Scottish pupils are to follow increasingly? The expected spread of subjects is normally English, history, geography, mathematics, science, music and art, technical subjects or domestic science, religious education, physical education—and a modern language. The reader may notice the deep breath drawn before the last mentioned item. It is in this area that the biggest staffing problems (especially in areas such as Shetland and Orkney) and the greatest difficulties in mixed ability teaching probably present themselves. In fact, the use of the mixed ability situation varies from subject to subject, since some teachers (more perhaps in the English-history-geography type of work) find themselves able to work with it, while in more 'linear' subjects such as French and mathematics, setting (or streaming into ability levels in one subject) tends to be more in use. There is also variation in timing for the start of setting, this depending to some extent on the length of the common course itself. One source of anxiety amongst teachers at the present time—or, more accurately, one source of disagreement—is the danger that the ablest pupils will be held back by the new organisation of classes. It is very obviously true, however, and has been experienced in other countries already, that the success or otherwise of the new regime depends very much on the personality, motivation, and work-philosophy of the teacher. A system stands or falls by its teachers. The 'commonness' of the course lies, in fact, in its

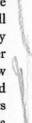

giving an initial equal opportunity to all pupils to cover the same
wide range of curriculum, and it is fully accepted that in time
an inevitable scatter of ability will emerge as with any human
group at any time. What is essential is that no 'labelling' takes
place, but that the pupils themselves should discover their
aptitudes and weaknesses, and hence be ripe for sensible choices
of subject at the age of fourteen, having received appropriate
guidance from the school staff.

Guidance is a field in which development is becoming very
necessary in the Scottish comprehensive school of the early
seventies. Many schools with a comprehensive history stretching back well before the 1965 national policy (especially in
Glasgow) have guidance counselling as a feature, but the total
picture is a patchy one. Now, however, the Scottish Education
Department and some local authorities, such as Aberdeenshire,
are pushing hard for the provision of this service in all schools,
and for training in counselling in the Colleges of Education. It is
evident that this frontier will be opened up in the next year or
two, and that this will be a prominent part of the transition to
comprehensive schooling by about 1975.

One aspect of the first two years remains to be discussed, that
of assessment. Although formal examinations are still very much
on the scene, their frequency is decreasing, and the idea of continuous assessment in various forms is making a limited appearance. This, however, is all that can be said at present, as no
significant experiment is under way in this direction.

YEARS THREE AND FOUR (14–16)

Schooling was compulsory only to fifteen until recently, but an
examination of the Scottish secondary school must now take into
account the raising of the final compulsory year to sixteen.
We shall therefore consider fourteen to sixteen as, for all practical purposes, the second, intermediate and, differentiated
phase of Scottish secondary school. It will readily be realised
that the whole of this account assumes a 2 + 2 + 2 format
within the six-year Scottish secondary; ie Common, Differentiated Compulsory, and Post-compulsory courses.

The greatest influence on the development of fourteen-to-sixteen education was the introduction of the O Grade Scottish Certificate of Education examination in fourth year in 1962. This meant that a far greater number of pupils completed education at sixteen than formerly. Now the leaving age is raised, it will in effect be compelling the attendance of only a minority, since pre-1972 the present trend had already created a willing majority of fifteen- and sixteen-year-olds under schooling. This increase in higher-level achievement has been one of the most telling arguments for the move to a comprehensive secondary pattern, since it seems to indicate that pupils should not be barred in any way from aiming as high as they can in even one of two O Grade courses. But in case the reader should get the impression that this examination has been the only force for change, it should be stressed that the twelve-to-fourteen common course had a definite effect on the structure of the fourteen-to-fifteen third secondary year, in that setting within subjects (rather than streaming by general ability) and 'bridging courses', combining a little certificate work with less academic material, gained ground as a general pattern. Generally, it is true that the change-over from a wide to a somewhat more directed course is tending to be made at the age of fourteen, but no rigid choices are implied, and transfer is always possible from course to course at this level should it prove necessary.

Some space must be devoted to the now famous (and certainly influential) Brunton Report of 1963 and its effect on the curriculum at the age level we are discussing. The essence of this Report's recommendations was that, for the less able pupils who were in great danger of finding school meaningless—especially if required to stay until sixteen—the curriculum should be organised around the 'vocational impulse'. By this was meant the interest the less able were assumed to have in the exciting world of adult work and the skills leading to effective participation therein. Basically, the Report suggested the provision of a range of courses (such as 'car-craft', building etc) which would in fact be work-based 'projects' to which all the traditional subjects would contribute but in a very non-traditional and meaningful way. This was in reality the Scottish 1960s version of 'education for life' in an industrial society. This has led in recent years to some very energetic, highly organised provision for fourteen- to sixteen-year-olds in some counties, particularly in the central industrial belt under local authorities such as Renfrewshire. (The reader who is interested in detail should read the second of two essays under the title 'Forward from Brunton' contained in the 1969 publication *Scottish Education Looks Ahead*, listed in the bibliography.)

However, the Report has been criticised for creating a picture of a pupil for whom work is the only exciting and meaningful thing in the world. Much has been said about the need for education geared to leisure and social/moral problems, especially in the last two years of compulsory schooling. In 1966, the follow-up publication of the Scottish Education Department *Raising the School Leaving Age*, took national thinking a stage further in suggesting the idea of three elements for courses at this level: (a) the 'Bruntonesque' vocational, (b) social and moral education and (c) leisure education. To revert to Renfrewshire as an example of the situation in 1969 after these two reports had their combined effect, it is laid down in that county that no more than 75 per cent of any pupil's time is to be occupied by the vocational element. Thus the other two elements were regarded as 'having a place'. A 'Progress Report' of the SED in 1970 shows that this place is growing rapidly. First, there has been an increase in the schools in recent years of a wide and varied menu of 'leisure and recreation' courses organised by physical education, music, art and other departments, of increasing use of outdoor centres, residential schools, camps, and so forth. The 1970 Report also indicates a slow extension of mixed academic/non-academic courses. Secondly, and more recently, there has arisen a specific interest in moral education as a part of the secondary school curriculum. The national committee concerned with religious and moral education issued its report in early 1972 and Aberdeen County lately published its own directive to its teachers on moral education. It is safe to assume that the fourteen-to-sixteen level will be a prime target for this sort of effort, if teachers can be persuaded to participate effectively, and this will demand courage. As the pattern of society changes to one of increasing automation, with shorter working hours, social/moral and leisure education will become increasingly important for the fourteen- to sixteen-year-olds, and not only for the less academic but for all of them. Scottish educational thinking is beginning to stress the importance of 'leisure-based and morality-oriented' curricula for the certificate and pre-university pupils as well— those for whom there is less of a vocational problem, who in Scottish educational tradition have been so successfully oriented vocationally as to remain underdeveloped in other ways.

Earlier remarks on the subject of counselling and guidance for the twelve-to-fourteen group are likely to apply equally to this phase of schooling also as it becomes universal in the 70s. The greater the variety of available courses, the more vital will counselling be to the effective working of the future Scottish comprehensive secondary school.

We began this section with the O Grade; let us finish by mentioning it again. The maximum number of subjects thought advisable in 1967 for a pupil was six (ie taking up no more than 75 per cent of class time). This covers the number of passes required for most forms of employment. It will be interesting to see if there is any increase not only in the percentage of pupils capable of achieving this number, but also in those capable of achieving even one pass. The decision on whether to expand and diversify the O Grade or to construct a new examination (see p 73) may well rest on this latter percentage.

YEARS FIVE AND SIX (16–18)

Already more pupils are staying on in these years in Scottish schools, as in most other industrially advanced countries with a growing demand for continued education as opposed to day-release training. It is inevitable that numbers will rise within the remaining thirty years of the century, at least to the present level in Scandinavia, and perhaps later to that in the USA and Japan. Since we may be taken by surprise at the rapidity of this climb the time is ripe for forward thinking about the structure of this educational stage, its content and its objectives.

It would be advisable, however, before speculating over the future, to look at the present situation. What has already been said previously should have made it clear that there is (a) a broad range of SCE Higher possibilities in fifth year, and (b) a growing number of subjects for the Certificate of Sixth Year Studies in the last year of schooling. What has not yet been explained is that a certain flexibility is possible, and that not every kind of flexibility possible has in fact been tried.

For instance, it is a common pattern at present in Scotland for a pupil to take some of the Higher passes he or she requires in the fifth year and some in the sixth year. Again some able fifth-year pupils may be examined for the first time in a subject at Higher level, or they may take the subject at Higher level having 'insured' themselves by an O Grade pass in fourth year. The use of O Grade as an 'insurance policy' depends on the individual headmaster's advice to pupil and parents, and on whether this advice is followed. In fact, one of the rather unexpected results of the O Grade's introduction in 1962 was its large-scale use as a stepping stone to the Higher—but perhaps this is simply another expression of Scottish character in Scottish educational langauge.

The hope, expressed in the annual report of the Secretary of State on Scottish education in 1964, that consideration should be given to the extent to which sixth-year pupils might be involved in working for O Grade passes in their 'minority time' studies, does not appear to have borne any fruit in Scotland generally. This is a very different position from that shown in the largely English 1970 report *Half Way There* (Benn and Simon) as prevailing throughout the many and varied sixth-form and sixth-form college patterns of English local authorities, where a sizeable percentage often work for such qualifications from sixteen to eighteen. To put it another way, there is a strong tendency (shown statistically by Benn and Simon) for Scottish schools to regard O Grade as a prerequisite for entry to the sixteen-to-eighteen phase, while this is not so in England. All these remarks apply to majority percentages in each case, and not to the small minority out of line with national patterns.

To complete the picture, O Grade *does* feature increasingly in the fifth year more than it does in the sixth, since at this stage it is not an 'extra' for those broadening a study range, but very often a pass they did not achieve at the expected time in the fourth, and therefore part of a 'catching-up' process like that established in England.

Comment has already been made (see p 65) on the possible future of the Certificate of Sixth Year Studies and the unsuccessful attempt to import the A Grade examination to Scotland. The expansion, or rather explosion, we must expect in the population of this sector of schooling may well bring far-reaching changes.

We began this section of our discussion by examining the thread of expanding demand for education which characterises this senior secondary phase. Some idea of the pre-1972 demand in Scotland is shown by the table (on pp 78–9). This shows pupils remaining at both local authority and grant-aided schools in Scotland, according to 1969 statistics, at ages 16, 17 and 18 as percentages of the age-group they themselves formed three, four or five years previously at age 13. The difference between the most urban and the most rural areas can readily be seen. Glasgow's local-authority schools show some of the lower percentages, and Sutherlandshire and Bute some of the highest, of those staying on at school.

Also, the vast difference between most local-authority schools and the grant-aided stands out clearly: for instance in Edinburgh's grant-aided schools, 92·3 per cent of the age sixteen intake stay on, as opposed to 30·5 per cent in state schools; in Glasgow, 88 as against 25·6 per cent, and in Perth and Kinross 91·5 as against 32·4. And in those same areas there are from 3–4 to 4–5 times as many in grant-aided schools at age of eighteen.

Pupil Democracy   International comparison indicates that an inevitable end-product of an enlarged sixteen-plus population is the need to create a structure of staff/student co-operation and student participation in matters affecting the running of the

Pupils remaining at education authority and grant-aided schools beyond the statutory leaving age, as percentages of the equivalent 13-year-old age groups 3/4/5 years previously

Percentages

Education authority area			16			Ages at 1st January 1969 — 17			18 and over		
			Boys	Girls	Boys and Girls	Boys	Girls	Boys and Girls	Boys	Girls	Boys and Girls
Burghs											
Aberdeen	E.A.	1	27·6	29·0	28·3	18·6	21·1	19·9	4·5	2·3	3·5
	G.A.	2	78·7	95·4	85·7	65·9	59·5	63·3	10·7	7·0	9·0
	Total	3	33·4	34·5	33·9	24·3	24·2	24·3	5·2	2·8	4·0
Dundee	E.A.	4	28·2	29·0	28·6	17·0	11·9	14·5	4·6	1·4	3·0
	G.A.	5	95·8	88·1	91·3	76·5	64·0	70·3	7·3	8·8	8·0
	Total	6	25·6	31·7	28·4	19·2	13·9	16·6	4·7	1·5	3·2
Edinburgh	E.A.	7	31·6	29·5	30·5	17·7	16·9	17·3	4·0	2·9	3·4
	G.A.	8	94·7	87·6	92·3	77·9	62·0	72·8	17·9	4·8	14·0
	Total	9	41·2	34·1	37·7	26·2	20·4	23·5	6·1	3·0	4·6
Glasgow	E.A.	10	26·9	24·3	25·6	16·8	11·7	14·3	4·2	2·2	3·2
	G.A.	11	90·4	85·8	88·0	65·3	55·4	60·3	10·3	10·9	10·6
	Total	12	29·5	27·2	28·4	18·8	13·6	16·2	4·4	2·5	3·5
Counties											
Dunbarton	E.A.	13	30·7	34·6	32·6	21·7	17·9	19·8	4·4	2·6	3·5
	G.A.	14	—	61·8	61·8	—	53·7	53·7	—	5·0	5·0
	Total	15	30·7	35·1	32·9	21·7	18·9	20·3	4·4	2·7	3·6
Lanark	E.A.	16	27·0	25·8	26·4	16·4	12·3	14·4	3·2	1·4	2·3
Renfrew	E.A.	17	29·9	28·6	29·2	19·3	13·6	16·4	3·7	1·3	2·6
	G.A.	18	—	95·7	95·7	—	43·8	43·8	—	4·7	4·7

No.											
23	E.A.	Clackmannan	0·8	—	1·5	9·7	8·5	11·0	21·1	22·0	20·2
24	G.A.		17·0	5·7	23·7	68·6	50·0	79·7	91·2	91·2	91·2
25	Total		2·9	0·6	4·9	17·7	12·7	22·8	30·2	29·4	31·0
26	E.A.	Fife	2·5	1·4	3·6	14·8	13·2	16·3	27·1	28·0	28·0
27	E.A.	Midlothian	2·7	3·0	2·4	12·9	10·9	14·8	24·4	24·8	24·0
28	E.A.	Stirling	1·9	1·2	2·5	13·7	12·2	15·0	26·0	24·8	27·1
29	E.A.	West Lothian	1·1	0·4	1·9	13·4	10·7	16·0	24·7	23·6	25·8
30	E.A.	Aberdeen	2·5	1·8	3·1	15·3	16·2	14·5	25·0	25·6	24·5
31	E.A.	Angus	1·1	0·8	1·3	12·9	13·5	12·2	26·8	26·2	27·4
32	E.A.	Banff	2·0	0·8	3·1	14·8	14·6	15·0	30·4	31·3	29·4
33	E.A.	Berwick	2·8	0·7	4·7	15·0	14·9	15·1	32·4	38·1	27·2
34	E.A.	Bute	5·1	4·0	5·8	24·4	30·9	18·1	41·9	35·9	46·2
35	E.A.	Dumfries	2·3	1·6	3·5	14·5	13·5	15·6	22·7	25·9	19·5
36	G.A.		29·0	5·6	34·7	62·9	87·5	57·5	64·2	73·1	61·9
37	Total		4·1	1·3	6·7	17·8	15·3	20·0	26·4	27·8	25·1
38	E.A.	East Lothian	2·5	1·7	3·4	15·9	10·7	21·9	27·7	26·9	28·5
39	E.A.	Kincardine	5·4	3·9	6·8	22·7	25·9	19·5	32·0	36·5	26·9
40	E.A.	Kirkcudbright	2·1	2·3	1·8	14·3	15·8	12·9	32·0	30·2	33·9
41	E.A.	Moray and Nairn	2·2	1·4	2·9	20·3	18·4	22·1	32·8	33·7	31·8
42	E.A.	Orkney	2·7	1·4	4·0	18·5	19·0	17·9	34·7	38·7	31·1
43	E.A.	Perth and Kinross	2·8	1·6	3·9	21·3	21·6	21·1	32·4	35·0	29·8
44	G.A.		11·7	4·3	16·9	67·0	62·0	71·7	91·5	92·7	90·6
45	Total		3·3	1·8	4·7	24·1	23·9	24·2	35·5	37·6	33·4
46	E.A.	Roxburgh	2·2	0·7	3·7	17·4	18·8	16·0	27·9	27·9	27·8
47	E.A.	Selkirk	4·5	1·8	7·1	21·0	18·2	23·9	36·2	32·1	40·5
48	E.A.	Wigtown	3·8	3·2	4·2	19·9	22·9	16·9	33·9	37·8	29·7
49	E.A.	Argyll	4·6	3·2	6·1	22·3	22·1	24·5	34·6	35·9	33·2
50	E.A.	Caithness	4·8	3·1	6·5	18·9	16·1	21·8	26·5	22·9	30·2
51	E.A.	Inverness	3·7	2·7	4·6	20·3	20·2	20·5	34·1	33·9	34·2
52	E.A.	Peebles	7·1	8·3	6·0	21·1	17·4	24·7	29·1	28·1	29·8
53	E.A.	Ross and Cromarty	4·6	2·6	6·6	20·8	20·4	21·3	36·9	42·9	30·5
54	E.A.	Sutherland	5·4	3·9	7·0	26·8	25·2	28·2	43·3	52·7	31·9
55	E.A.	Zetland	5·0	4·7	5·3	19·0	19·4	18·7	33·6	34·4	32·8
56	E.A.	Scotland	2·9	1·9	3·8	16·0	14·4	17·4	28·0	27·8	28·1
57	G.A.		12·0	7·2	15·7	63·0	56·4	68·0	85·3	84·6	85·8
58	Total		3·1	2·1	4·2	17·3	15·5	19·1	29·7	29·4	30·0

From: *Scottish Educational Statistics*, 1969.

school. At present most Scottish schools, with a fairly traditional
provision for an academic minority, still maintain some form
(perhaps as a consultative council) of the prefect system, differing
from school to school mainly in the degree of latitude allowed
the pupils by the headmaster in their choice or election of pre-
fects. This system works, of course, as well as the people involved
allow it to, but is on the whole less democratic than that which
will be demanded in future. Some form of school council will
almost certainly be a sine qua non of the Scottish secondary, and
not, as at the moment, something operated by *avant-garde* headmasters who are looked on with something approaching suspicion in more cautious quarters. The writer suggests that the
most fruitful source of ideas on this subject is Scandinavia,
Denmark particularly.

One trend which is certainly appearing in this school level,
however, is the greater encouragement to independent work and
study, and initiative in lines of work, which is being given to
school pupils by teachers, especially when they are free of 'the
Highers' in the sixth year. The occurrence of an examination in
the fifth year which tends to engender examination-oriented
work rather than independent critical thinking is something of an
obstacle to this, but the opportunity does come to a limited
number in the sixth to rise beyond examination demands—provided a large proportion of their curricular week is not occupied
with more Highers.

Sixth-form Colleges   Lastly, some space must be given to
the structural possibility of the sixth-form college or junior
college. In English local authorities this structure—either as a
separate form of upper academic school or as a newer form of
open entry upper secondary for the whole ability spectrum of
sixteen-plus—is quite widely used as one of the acceptable forms
of the comprehensive system. But in Scotland, most regrettably,
it has made its appearance only on paper as a suggestion for
future development—and this merely in a note of reservation by
one member of the Public Schools Commission in 1970—and
in national daily newspaper articles and discussion on education.
Perhaps the very fact that it was mentioned in a minority state-

ment of opinion in an official report is eloquent of its lack of prominence in Scotland. Naturally, since almost all Scottish local authorities have chosen the six-year secondary as the form of schooling to be adopted, it seems the less likely that this structure will appear. But changed circumstances may force its reconsideration, at least in certain Scottish areas. In the urban areas there are already signs that the all-through neighbourhood school (as past American experience should have warned) is not living up to its objectives socially because of drift to the suburbs by those who can choose their price for housing. The danger here is of a distinction being made between 'good' and 'bad' comprehensive schools. It is arguable that a more centralised upper tier of schooling, perhaps not at sixteen-plus because of possible disincentive in change of school at a bad time but at fourteen-plus (and this is why Stirlingshire's three-tier plan will prove interesting from 1973 onwards) would spread the provision on a more equitable basis to all sectors of the city area. Secondly, in the more sparsely populated rural area, a more satisfactorily sized fifth/sixth-year group might be created by bringing together those at this age level either in a centre of six-year schooling as a recognisably separate 'young adult' group, or separately in a new, carefully located spot, or perhaps both. In fact flexibility and rational planning should be as characteristic of Scottish local authorities as they have been of some English. Again the example of Scandinavia is particularly relevant to the Scottish rural area in that there, post-compulsory schooling is thought of as a necessarily 'different' phase of maturity. All kinds of provision are integrated at this level in fewer and larger centres in a way that is economical in staffing and resources as well as socially better in terms of residential facilities for those far from their families—facilities not on the whole needed by those below sixteen because of the careful organisation of compulsory schooling within reach of home. While one would not suggest the importation of the Swedish 'New Gymnasium', for instance, to a culturally different environment, the principles underlying its development require serious thought in Scottish terms.

Two points are relevant here. Firstly, the reorganised regional

F

authority which will result from the Wheatley Report on the reorganisation of local government in Scotland, the ensuing White Paper and subsequent legislation, is envisaged as the body responsible for the educational planning of the future. The years of the change-over to the new structure will also be the years of growth in the sixteen-to-eighteen group, and planning of six-teen-to-eighteen education will therefore certainly be one of the issues before the regions. The region will by its very nature replace or at least devalue irrationalities, local jealousies or lop-sided planning. It is therefore not impossible that such school-ing structures as have been described will be introduced, at least in some places.

Secondly, even if such structures do not emerge as practical politics, it is virtually certain to anyone looking south at develop-ments in the more urbanised English situation that many more links will be formed in the near future between the secondary school sixteen-to-eighteen group and the technical college part-time day-release group of the same age. This is already happen-ing south of the border, and Glasgow is doing a certain amount in this field. At the earlier fifteen-sixteen level the school began to take over some years ago, and the completion of the process is merely a matter of time in view of the recent extension of the leaving age to sixteen. In fact this has been the subject of official pronouncements by the Secretary of State for Scotland in recent months.

CURRICULAR DEVELOPMENTS IN THE SECONDARY SCHOOL

This is not the place to enter into technical details on the teaching of individual subjects, but our view of Scottish secondary schooling would be impaired if we paid no attention to the main developments in subject teaching

Mathematics teaching has undergone a great revolution in Scotland, as a result of the initiative taken by the Mathematics Syllabus Committee in the last few years. Developments are numerous in the direction of discovery, concept formation, practical applications to everyday life, introduction to hitherto untouched topics, programmed material, teachers' aids and a host of other means. The content of O Grade and Higher Mathematics has been transformed and modernised. Perhaps the most interesting feature is that the series *Modern Mathematics for Schools* (published by Blackie/Chambers) has achieved wide use in the rest of the United Kingdom, Eire, Scandinavia, Germany, Holland, South Africa and Australia. This is indeed a Scottish educational success.

English teaching has also moved far from the traditional. The emphasis now tends to be on the 'oracy' of the pupil, on linguistic competence and situational fluency, on individualised learning based on an ever increasing range of materials and technological 'hardware', and on the careful relating of literature to human problems and situations; the living dialect is given an enhanced status and there is less insistence on a 'correct BBC' standard of speech. Local teachers' centres and development groups have played a significant part in these reforms.

The sciences also now have a transformed and 'alternative' syllabus in most schools, affecting the content of examinations also. The main change here has been a swing towards the understanding of basic concepts rather than the learning of definitions and laws, and the careful inclusion in the teaching syllabus of the most modern scientific advances in the outside world. The objective is to plan a series of 'concept explorations' in such a way that comprehension will develop, judgement be exercised and theories grasped.

Modern languages also present an interesting and encouraging picture of change and modernisation after long adherence to tradition. Again, work right through to examination stage has an emphasis on oral fluency, language laboratories are in increasing use in schools and research is being done on the more effective teaching of modern languages to pupils in a mixed-ability situation, as in the years twelve to fourteen. Recently the formation of a National Steering Committee has given an impetus to all such changes. The spread of French teaching at primary level, even if slow because of lack of qualified staff, was one factor that made reconsideration of teaching method necessary.

In history, more importance is now given to study skill, to the use of evidence and to the 'patch' examination of a period or place in depth, rather than to factual knowledge and memorisation. In geography increased realism is the aim, and general concepts are arrived at by the study of examples. In the early stages of secondary teaching subjects are integrated into themes and the new modern studies (civics) gives an opportunity for work based on everyday life.

The study of economics, and of commercial studies generally, is growing in Scottish schools. Parallel to this, much more time is now given to liaison between education and industry, through encouragement by special local-authority officers appointed for this purpose.

Great expansion has been seen also in the musical and dramatic fields, in increased opportunities for instrumental playing and participation in theatre projects. Art syllabuses are also being revised by a current working party.

New physical education programmes are under way, and an interest is being taken in health education.

Finally, in the field of classical studies experiments are being carried out in the introduction of non-linguistic 'European' themes. There is a swing towards comprehension and away from translation, this being made possible by the use of programmed material of greater interest.

National centres for curriculum development (eg in English, mathematics/science, modern studies) have been, and are to be set up in colleges of education. One of the most recent to be planned is a modern languages centre in Aberdeen College.

The 1970s could be very adequately described as the new age of Scottish education. All that we have said applies not only to state education, but also to those secondary schools which lie outside local authority provision, in the grant-aided and independent sector—but more, of course, to the former than to the latter. A brief description of these non-state schools follows on pp 85–93, but first some idea of state school residential provision must be given.

STATE RESIDENTIAL FACILITIES

It is, of course, the case in Scotland that many secondary pupils in local authority secondary schools have, because of distance, to use hostels that are attached to the school and provided by the local authority, or to stay in foster homes. This is particularly so in the Highlands and Islands, where for a long time senior secondary pupils entering certificate courses have found hostels necessary from the age of twelve to seventeen/eighteen. Comprehensive education and the twelve-to-fourteen common course are introducing a trend in some areas to the postponement of 'hostelisation' until fourteen, especially in island areas; but this separation of child and family is still regarded as something of a problem and a factor in depopulation. In recent years, programmes of new hostel building have been initiated by the Scottish Education Department, with a much more informal 'family unit' atmosphere and approximation to home conditions, and the careful selection and training of suitably sympathetic and knowledgeable people as wardens. Research on the organisational and sociological aspects of hostel living is also being supported by the Department. These trends should be kept in mind by the reader during the following account of the private sector and the Public Schools Commission's recommendations on use of state and private boarding facilities.

GRANT-AIDED AND INDEPENDENT SCHOOLS

The *Second Report of the Public Schools Commission*, published in 1970, is a definitive source of detailed information. Volume 3 of the report deals very fully with the whole Scottish secondary education pattern, state and non-state schooling alike, since the Commission's brief from the Socialist government was to recommend the future pattern of state-private co-operation in detail and explore the ways in which the private sector would participate in the comprehensive policy of the regions where the schools happened to be located.

Of interest, perhaps, is the geographical distribution of non-state schools in Scotland (see p 86). This is, as the reader will

LOCATION OF GRANT-AIDED AND INDEPENDENT DAY SCHOOLS IN SCOTLAN

From: *Public Schools Commission, 2nd Report*, Vol 3

Grant-aided Schools: primary and secondary rolls
(with boarders) at January 1968

	Primary	Secondary	Total (Boarders shown in brackets)	
Aberdeen Albyn School for Girls	232	263	495	(60)
Convent of the Sacred Heart School	96	148	244	(79)
Robert Gordon's College	305	851	1,156	(54)
St. Margaret's School for Girls	166	217	383	(57)
Dundee The High School	544	601	1,145	
Edinburgh Daniel Stewart's College	443	498	941	(46)
George Watson's College	616	914	1,530	(97)
George Watson's Ladies' College	455	514	969	
Mary Erskine School for Girls	464	491	955	
George Heriot's School	579	926	1,505	
John Waton's School	221	212	433	(66)
Melville College	266	267	533	(31)
St. Mary's Cathedral Choir School	18	15	33	
Glasgow Craigholme School for Girls	355	224	579	
Hutcheson's Boys' Grammar School	237	633	870	
Hutcheson's Girls' Grammar School	254	627	881	
Kelvinside Academy	297	350	647	
Laurel Bank School	301	283	584	
St. Aloysius' College	279	558	837	
Westbourne School for Girls	311	324	635	
The Park School	246	260	506	
Helensburgh St. Bride's School	204	194	398	(115)
Kilmacolm St. Columba's School	246	207	453	(23)
Troon Marr College	—	808	808	
Dollar Dollar Academy	278	558	836	(234)
Maxwelltown Benedictine Convent School	45	112	157	
Dumfries St. Joseph's College	52	450	502	(350)
Crieff Morrison's Academy for Boys	123	301	424	(163)
Morrison's Academy for Girls	183	275	458	(97)
	7,816	12,081	19,879	(1,472)

Source: Questionnaires to schools.

From: *Public Schools Commission, 2nd Report*, Vol 3

The fourteen selected independent day schools:
Primary and Secondary rolls (with boarders) at January 1968

		Primary	Secondary	Total (Boarders shown in brackets)	
Edinburgh	Cranley School for Girls	112	148	260	(63)
	St. Denis School	219	236	455	(121)
	Edinburgh Academy	560	471	1,031	(152)
	St. George's School for Girls	334	305	639	(83)
	St. Hilary's School	132	146	278	(65)
	Lansdowne House	160	121	281	
	St. Margaret's Convent School	188	146	334	(48)
	St. Margaret's School for Girls (Newington)	225	221	446	(58)
	St. Serf's School for Girls	75	89	164	
	Scotus Academy	103	198	301	
	Rudolf Steiner School	193	124	317	
Glasgow	Glasgow Academy	348	596	944	(39)
Ayr	Wellington School	151	268	419	(109)
Bridge of Allan	Beacon School	121	141	262	(102)
		2,921	3,210	6,131	(840)

Source: Questionnaires to schools and returns to Scottish Education Department.

From: *Public Schools Commission, 2nd Report*, Volume 3.

see, predominantly central and urban; although some schools
are found in the more populated and pleasant central highlands, there are none at all in the Highlands and Islands proper.
The earlier historical account (pp 14 and 18) goes far towards ex-
plaining this.

The two categories of the private sector are (a) the grant-aided
and (b) the independent schools. Let us sketch in the essentials
of each to give a little perspective.

The grant-aided schools   In the grant-aided sector (corre-

sponding in some but not all respects to the English direct grant)
there are 29 schools which receive financial aid from the Scottish
Education Department towards costs. The list of these can be
seen in detail in the table on p 87. Of the 29, there are 11 for
boys, 14 for girls and 4 co-educational; they follow no set pattern,
the smallest containing fewer than 40 pupils of a middle-school
range and the largest about 1,600 in the full primary-secondary
range. Almost all are primary-secondary establishments, with a
tendency towards social selectivity. However, one, Marr College
in Troon (incidentally also the only one with a purely secondary
population), does not charge fees and is already effectively the
comprehensive school for its area. The Roman Catholic Church
runs four and the Scottish Episcopal Church one of these schools.
Their histories vary in length from 322 to 37 years at the time of
writing.

Aid was until 1923 given in a haphazard way, then rationalised
for a truncated list of 16 schools which, increased by two and
decreased by three transfers to state control, became 15. This
was the number receiving aid in 1959 when the present general
grant arrangements came into force for these 15, together with
14 former independent schools, making the current total of 29.
Until recently the amount of grant was 'the approved deficit on
maintenance costs up to 60 per cent of approved expenditure, no
grant being payable on capital expenditure' (*Second Report of
the Public Schools Commission*, Vol 3, paragraph 4.18). To receive
grant, they must conform to state school legal requirements,
pay at least minimum state salaries and observe all that is laid
down in the Schools (Scotland) Code. Normally they have their
own management, in most cases singly, but sometimes three or
four schools come under one control, the best known example
perhaps being the Merchant Company schools of Edinburgh.
These management boards often have local authority or university representation.

All except two of the schools charge fees, those being the
already-mentioned Marr College and the one Episcopal school,
St Mary's Cathedral Choir School, Edinburgh. The fees range
from £38 to £140 per annum on the most recent available

figures. Teachers must have state levels of qualification and registration, and the teacher/pupil ratio is usually good, although not uniformly so in all grant-aided schools.

As a group they deal with about 23,000 of the 950,000 in Scotland's primary and secondary population; this is about 1 in 40 of the total. It has already been noted that they have vastly greater holding power than state schools in the sixteen-to-eighteen range, which is only to be expected from parentally well-supported institutions. Selection procedures vary from none at all to written tests, and include admission of younger siblings, preference for children of former pupils and scholarship awards. Since over 50 per cent of these schools have a fairly wide IQ range, while about 30/40 per cent draw three-quarters of their intake from the IQ range of 110-plus, they resemble different types of schools in the state sector. As to social class, about 80 per cent of the pupils are reported to come from Social Class I (professional), most of the remaining 20 per cent from Class II (supervisory manual, clerical etc) and a very few from III, IV and V (skilled, partly-skilled and unskilled occupations). Usually they prepare for the normal range of Scottish external state examinations, but some aim at other targets such as Oxford/ Cambridge entrance.

The independent schools   The number of independent schools (other than 'public schools)' is around the 130 mark, and they contain about 15,000 of the school population in Scotland but only a little over 3,000 secondary pupils. In other words very few have secondary departments, and the rest—strictly speaking —constitute a primary school private sector. Generally a three-tier pattern is evident: roughly, five to nine; nine to fourteen (preparatory); fourteen to eighteen (public/secondary). Reference to the map and table on p 88 will show the 14 day schools which have over 100 secondary pupils, and the striking fact that 11 out of the 14 are in Edinburgh.

In addition to these independent schools, there are 10 'public schools' (in the English sense of affiliation to the Headmasters' Conference attended by Eton, Harrow and like schools) and, taken together, public and independent cater for a segment of the school population roughly equal to that in the grant-aided schools. Of the 140 or so schools, over 50 are boarding establishments and the rest are day schools (ie boarding is provided by both 'public' and 'non-public' independent schools).

Historically, the independent sector is of no older vintage than the first quarter of the nineteenth century, this applying equally to 'public' and 'non-public' independent, and geographically is concentrated in Edinburgh. If the reader collates this fact with earlier information on feepaying local authority schools in Edinburgh, and looks at the map of the independent and grant-aided schools (p 86), he will have no difficulty in realising the uniqueness of Edinburgh in Scottish education. Neither will the complexity of educational status levels in that city escape him.

Little use is now made of local authority power to finance places for pupils in the grant-aided sector or to help provide facilities for such schools in their area (in contrast to English 'direct grant'). In general, independent schools almost entirely pay their own way, their day pupils' fees ranging from £95 to £180 approximately in primary, and from £120 to £225 in secondary schools. They are, however, subject to state inspection even if insistence on 'efficiency' is not backed by law as in England, but examinations and teaching qualifications are not subject to the same controls as in grant-aided schools. Social background range is almost exactly as in grant-aided, and selectivity ranges from high to medium academic ability. Their equipment varies vastly in quality.

The future of the private sector   What of the future of the private sector? The main fact to be kept in mind is that the First and Second Reports of the Public Schools Commission were produced during the last period of Socialist government, and that they were motivated by a Socialist desire to integrate the state and private sectors to some degree. We do not know what the future implementation of these recommendations will be. One would tend to expect less of a desire on the part of a Conservative government to weld together state and private sectors. In fact, the indications at the committee stage of the Education

(Scotland) Bill, through which, in 1971, the government moved painfully slowly, were that feepaying was to be reintroduced in former local authority feepaying schools. If this is to be done *within* the state sector, the implication would seem to be retention of the *status quo* in the state-private relationship. Despite all this, however, it is hard to imagine that the work of a Commission representing university, local authority and other interests as well as those of both state and private schools will be allowed permanently to gather dust on the shelf. It represents, after all, a fair consensus of opinion on the possible way forward from the present situation, and the Conservative government, whose policy is by no means dedicated to the reversal of progress made so far, may well wish to consider in the light of these reports what state-private links can be established.

The Scotsman report of 27 March 1971 seems, however, to indicate that the present Conservative government does not regard the Commission's proposals as objective, and that it proposes a re-examination of the problem and retention of grant aid.

The Commission's more important recommendations for Scottish schooling were briefly these:

1. a comprehensive role for all state schools
2. no state feepaying, as inconsistent with the comprehensive principle
3. free choice of state schools provided each school contains a cross-section of social class
4. positive discrimination in favour of deprived-area schools in terms of re-zoning, resources and publicity
5. grant-aided schools to act as components of one-, two- or three-tier comprehensive systems as their structure fits them
6. private school roles to be settled by bilateral negotiation
7. reorganised public representation on private governing bodies
8. grant aid to cease after role is settled (ie state integration)
9. new financing plans either by local authority or under a

Scottish School Grants Committee (cf University Grants Committee)

10. new building to be approved by the Secretary of State as part of local authority plans
11. two to three years for discussion of new roles
12. schools unwilling to participate free to choose independent status (veiled threat of increased fees, increased social selectivity and economic demise?) over a five-year transition period of grant reduction
13. present freedoms of schools to be retained as far as participation allows
14. independent schools to be *invited* to similar participation in state system
15. residential education to be equitably shared out
16. tuition to be free for all

THE STATE SECONDARY AS AN ORGANISATION

As state comprehensive secondaries grow in size, they present administrative problems not found in smaller and less flexible schools, so that the headmaster, who should be the philosopher-king and policy-maker, is in danger of becoming bogged down in clerical/secretarial detail, timetabling and other tasks. He also may have few contacts with his large student body.

Pioneer work has been done by the Edinburgh Corporation education authority on administration and management in secondary schools, the gist of which is that the teaching staff—and especially the head—should be freed from time-wasting tasks by the appointment of administrative officers, already a feature of the Edinburgh school scene. The timetable of the school, for instance, is one of the tasks that should be done by the administrative officer—and with the help of the computer.

The size of the new comprehensives, of course, implies the use of the guidance counsellors discussed earlier. It could mean their appointment as 'assistant headmasters'—a new middle-level executive grade in the secondary-school business.

Lastly, one may guess that all future headmasters of large

schools will have to undergo a form of in-service training using 'simulated decision situations', a method employed long ago by the armed services and in fact already in use to some extent in courses for primary and secondary headmasters, although such courses do not yet lead automatically to promotion.

5

Special, further and higher education

SPECIAL SCHOOLING FOR THE HANDICAPPED

IT is the duty of local authorities to provide special education for handicapped children between the ages of five and sixteen who come under any of the nine officially recognised categories. This has been the case since legislation to this effect in 1946, and the Acts of 1962 and 1969 define the position even more precisely.

The local authority must ascertain, through its educational psychologists, medical staff and teachers, which children are in need of various types of special schooling, and it has powers to make a parent submit his child for examination, if necessary. If the need for special schooling is established, the medical officer will, if required, sign a certificate to that effect. As in other educational matters, the parent has the right of appeal to the Secretary of State against the decision (which is taken in conjunction with the health authority).

The nine recognised categories of handicap under 1954 Regulations, and Circular 300 1955 are: (i) the mentally handicapped, (ii) the physically handicapped, (iii) the deaf, (iv) the partially deaf, (v) the partially sighted, (vi) the maladjusted, (vii) the blind, (viii) epileptics, (ix) spastics.

Something under 11,000 of Scotland's children attend special schools, 'occupational centres' or local health authority 'care centres', which cater respectively for 'educable' (IQ 55–70), 'trainable' (IQ 40–55) and 'untrainable' (below IQ 40). As has been pointed out many times, these IQ levels are no more than a rough guide for making a humane decision based on knowledge of the individual.

Special education straddles both public and grant-aided sectors in over 140 schools, and is provided in four types of school or class: (i) day special schools, (ii) residential schools, (iii) residential-cum-day schools, (iv) special classes in ordinary schools. Most of the large mentally handicapped group find themselves in some form of day provision, while most of those with physical handicap or maladjustment are under residential care. In other groups provision varies as to type of school. Blind children, however, are to be found in one institution, the Royal Blind School in Edinburgh, as the easiest and most efficient form of provision.

About two-thirds of all handicapped schoolchildren in Scotland are mentally handicapped and roughly one-eighth physically handicapped; the next biggest group is of deaf children (over 400); and then follow the partially deaf (over 300), the partially sighted and maladjusted (each over 200), the blind (over 100), and the rest in double figures.

What of present trends? The indications are that building programmes are under way in urban and rural areas alike to provide new special schools and occupational centres, particularly for the mentally and physically handicapped, residentially and centrally in the latter case. Needs for improvement in forecasting incidence, in ascertainment (although the 1969 Act has gone in this direction), in testing and in after-care are evident. More liaison with industry and provision of occupational opportunities for the physically handicapped require investigation, and residential education for the maladjusted is likely to receive greater attention through curriculum development, in-service training for teacher-counsellors and so on. A very good source of information about advances made in Scottish special education is the essay by H. B. Jones on the subject in *Scottish Education Looks Ahead* (see bibliography, p 135), in which, in addition to covering some topics introduced above, he mentions such potential growth points as: (i) the necessity in the twelve-to-sixteen age range to bring the curriculum nearer to normal secondary provision, as a better preparation for ordinary life; (ii) increasing placement of the formerly 'untrainable' in occupational centres and the need to review training for the staff in charge of them; (iii) the need for special education to adapt flexibly and continuously to the increase or decrease in various handicaps, and to take medical advance into account; (iv) the use of educational technology and the oral approach with the growing deaf group; (v) the special problem of the smallness of the blind group and the need to provide for them a better secondary level curriculum centrally and residentially; (vi) the emergence of newly diagnosed forms of handicap such as communication disorder and autism and the need for flexibility in provision to meet such needs; (vii) the need for clearer definitions of maladjustment and delinquency, for expansion of the Child Guidance Services at present run by many local authorities (in which ideally a trio of psychologist, psychiatrist and psychiatric social worker deal with individual cases of personality disorder, educational backwardness, habitual delinquent behaviour etc referred to them by school, parent, medical service or other agencies) and for greater provision of 'approved schools' for residential education of such children.

FURTHER EDUCATION

To give a short account of this area of Scottish education is a problem indeed! However, some guidelines to more detailed reading can at least be laid down.

The term 'further' includes (a) education or training (part-time or full-time) which leads to vocational or job qualifications for those beyond the age of compulsory schooling; (b) adult education of the formal evening class type provided over a vast range of subjects, with no thought of qualification or employment but merely for interest and self-improvement; (c) provision through voluntary organisations and local education authorities of recreational, social, physical and youth club facilities— obviously the least controlled and most miscellaneous of these three sub-areas. It is with the first of the three—the 'vocational' —that most of our time in this section must be taken.

G

Vocational   Vocational further education is dominated by its two main sectors—technical and commercial—and fast-expanding technical education has perhaps the first call upon our attention.

Technical education takes place on a variety of levels: technological universities (Heriot Watt in Edinburgh, and Strathclyde in Glasgow), central institutions (a range of technical, art, music, domestic science, agricultural and nautical colleges falling within the administrative responsibility of Scottish Education Department or Department of Agriculture), and colleges of further education serving the total area, or sub-areas of local authorities. The two universities were formerly also central institutions, three in number, two of which were combined in Glasgow. Others no doubt will eventually be given university status. Generally the higher level qualifications—degrees, associateships and Higher National Diploma (HND)—are provided in the universities and central institutions, while the colleges of further education deal with day-release (the most general form of course), block-release, apprenticeship, sandwich and similar courses ending in qualifications such as Ordinary National Diplomas (OND), Higher National and Ordinary National Certificates (HNC and ONC), and awards of the City and Guilds of London Institute (CGLI). Official recognition is given to four types of industrial job for which technical education is designed:

1. Technologist   Degree, degree-level, associateship (separate or leading to a degree of the Council for National Academic Awards) course of four years, or three-year courses for Higher National Diploma.

2. Technician   Two-year part-time courses for ONC (entry level three O Grades), HNC (entry ONC); also two-year full-time 'sandwich' courses for OND (entry level four O Grades), and three-year courses for HND (entry level appropriate SCE Highers and O Grades, or appropriate ONC or OND).

3. Craftsman   Two- to three-year courses for CGLI Craft

Certificate (attainment of age 16 for entry), and two- to three-year courses for CGLI Advanced Certificate (entry level Craft Certificate).

4. Operative   Courses of varying lengths, for CGLI Craft Certificate (if any).

The range of studies at all levels covers all skills and sectors of industry, the objectives being in (1) to produce leaders in the engineering and technological fields, in (2) technologists' aides and supervisors of skilled men, in (3) competent skilled men, and in (4) competent machine operators and process workers. In addition, a range of courses designed to adjust the fifteen-to-sixteen age group have been provided (this may be an obsolescent) feature in view of extended compulsory education.

The Scottish Technical Education Consultative Council, which exists to co-ordinate the above provision under the Industrial Training Act of 1964 has (mid-1971) published an interesting Report. It proposes, with backing from the Secretary of State for Scotland, the rationalisation of the above complexity (a) by setting up of a new body, the Scottish Technical Education Council (SCOTEC) and (b) the replacement of existing parallel courses (eg HNC and CGLI) by a single co-ordinated framework.

Commercial education constitutes the second most important sector of job-based further education. Here the controlling body is the Scottish Council for Commercial, Administrative and Professional Education, and, in general, provision of courses is confined to colleges of further education. However, central institutions do cater for students to enter training as teachers of commerce, and the University of Strathclyde's School of Business and Administration has a BA degree for teachers of commerce. Commercial courses on the following lines are available:

1. Aspects of office work (entry age 15) usually a two-year course leading to a certificate.
2. Secretarial courses, based on O Grade or Higher English or previous secretarial certificates and leading to secretarial or advanced secretarial certificates after two years' part-time study.

3. Scottish National Diploma in Business Studies (two years full-time) and Scottish National Certificate in Business Studies (two years' part-time) based on four Ordinary Grade passes including English.
4. Scottish Advanced National Certificate in Business Studies based on possession of National Certificate or an equivalent qualification.
5. One-year and half-year courses for graduates.

Unlike other spheres of education in Scotland, training of teachers in technical and commercial education is by no means universal yet. Training for technical teachers is given centrally on a sandwich basis in Jordanhill College of Education, Glasgow; the training of commercial teachers, has already been touched on.

It seems certain that in the very near future many curricular links will be formed between schools and colleges of further education so that the 15/16–18 group may take courses unavailable in their own institution. Recent consultation among local authorities point in this direction, and examples of such schemes are already to be found in England.

Adult education and youth work   The adult and social/recreational areas of the sector under discussion can be quickly dealt with. First, the provision of adult education is expanding to meet ever-increasing demand. In this, local education authorities co-operate closely with the extra-mural departments of universities to provide an annually wider range of subjects—from philosophy to handicrafts, from archaeology to psychology, and 1,001 topics between. The Workers' Educational Association also plays its traditional role in providing classes of all kinds for those who wish to raise their own cultural level. In some secondary-school centres, especially in suburban areas, the length of class-enrolment queues has provided good copy for local newspapers.

There is still little emphasis on adult education for the attainment of qualifications by a 'second-chance method'. What exists of this (eg the achievement of 'Highers' for university entrance) tends to be found in centres of further education such as commercial colleges. The expansion of this concept can, however, be confidentially predicted through the influence of the international idea of 'lifelong education'. Some attempt has been made to import the Scandinavian folk high school theme into Scottish adult education, which has only one real residential centre in the Edinburgh area so far, and plans for a Celtic folk high school in the outer Hebrides have been discussed. A predictable growth point for adult education in the future is, of course, the now operational 'University of the Air'—the national television or 'Open University'.

As far as social, recreational and youth-work education are concerned, again the keynote is expansion. The local authority's provision of youth-club facilities (and increasingly of secondary-school 'youth wings') exists hand-in-glove with close supervision given by the appropriate branch of the Scottish Education Department. Recent years have also seen co-operation by most of the traditional voluntary youth organisations in a national Standing Conference framework; and through the co-operation of colleges of education, regional training organisations which are representative of both voluntary and state interests have been set up on the lines suggested in two reports of the Kilbrandon Council. Moray House College in Edinburgh and Jordanhill College in Glasgow have also led the way in providing professional training for youth leaders.

UNIVERSITIES AND COLLEGES OF EDUCATION

Our initial historical account (pp 31–3) showed these sectors as they have developed up to the present day; therefore the objective here is to clarify contemporary trends.

Broadly, contemporary higher education is divisible in Scotland into three parts—the universities, the colleges of education, and the central institutions, which could respectively be categorised as general higher, teacher preparation, and higher technical education preparatory to professions other than teaching. The central institutions were dealt with in our section on further education. They could in fact be regarded as the higher-education level of further education, leading as described to degrees, diplomas and associateships: in other words, it is impossible to think in watertight compartments when describing the sectors of Scottish education. We shall deal here mainly with the other two components, universities and colleges of education, which lie totally within the higher education level, and between which links have begun to be forged. We are dealing, it may be added, with the clearly separable 'post-Robbins era' in British higher education, the years since the publication in 1963 of the Robbins Report on Higher Education, which dealt in proportion, and with due regard to national variations, with Scottish higher education.

The universities of the post-Robbins era   From 1964 to 1967 the university pattern in Scotland was transformed. The four traditional universities of St Andrews, Aberdeen, Glasgow and Edinburgh were joined by two rather different pairs: (a) Strathclyde University in Glasgow and Heriot Watt in Edinburgh, both formerly central institutions and now 'technological universities', (b) Dundee University, formerly an offshoot of St Andrews and now with full status and of rather different pattern from its mother institution, and Stirling, the only completely new creation in Scotland with some exciting new objectives and a growing student body.

While the universities are not, strictly speaking, a form of state education, they can be said to approximate very closely to it. Over four-fifths of university finance comes from central government, controlled, channelled and advised upon in five-year phases by the University Grants Committee, a body representative of academic, school and research interests. This money is furnished both on an ad hoc basis for plant and facilities, and on a quinquennial pattern for general expenditure, the plans of individual universities being taken into account. The second type of finance is a good example of British compromise, since amounts for individual institutions are controlled from the centre while spending priorities are at the discretion of the receiving university, so that a measure of cherished autonomy is retained.

University entrance qualification is an important consideration in the study of any national education system. In Scotland, until 1968, entrance requirements were fixed by the Scottish Universities Entrance Board, and its Attestation of Fitness, relevant to the four traditional universities, was a prerequisite to entry to any of the four. But in 1968 the separate existence of two technological (and therefore specialised) universities, two general foundations not committed to this national pattern, and the increasing tendency of the traditional four themselves to apply varying standards even among faculties, made it clear that the Attestation was no longer relevant. Both Attestation and Board were abolished, and the Scottish Universities Council on Entrance now deals, broadly speaking, with national matters of this sort.

As to the main characteristics of university courses, faculties have expanded beyond the traditional into the applied and social science areas particularly, but the emphasis on retaining generality and breadth in higher education (in contrast to the English universities) has remained, in that the three-year Ordinary degree of MA or BSc still is a strong option for a goodly proportion of students, probably about one in three in the case of Arts Faculty entrants. Medicine as yet requires six years; dentistry and veterinary science five. New types of degree are provided by Stirling (BA Ordinary or Honours in Arts, Science or Combined Arts/Science, and new combined Honours courses in Arts or Science or Social Science combined with education and teaching practice for teaching, and in technological economics for the business world and governmental careers). Strathclyde provides a new BA Ordinary or Honours degree in Arts and Social Studies etc. Also the new Ordinary degree in education, the four-year BEd, is offered by universities and colleges of education in partnership as a combination of university study and teacher training. The first of these students (three women) graduated in Aberdeen in 1968, and rapid expansion in numbers has followed.

University teaching methods—and this applies to colleges of education too—have moved very much away from the lecture to the use of small group techniques such as the seminar and tutorial, the need for this having been highlighted by the Hale

Report of 1964. Numbers of students at Scottish universities—
undergraduate and postgraduate, men and women—and a breakdown of types of study can be seen on the tables set out on pp
105–9. The fact that just over three-fifths of these students came
from state schools, and about one-fifth each from grant-aided and
independent schools may be of additional interest to the reader
when considered against the background of the earlier account
of the secondary school structure (pp 67–9, 85–93), showing as it
did 2·5 per cent of Scotland's secondary school pupils in grant-
aided and about 0·33 per cent in independent schools. The future
will certainly see an increased flow from state schools into higher
education.

An inquiry conducted for the Robbins Committee (1963)
showed (a) that university staff in Scotland spend about one-third
of their working time on average on each of the two major
functions of teaching and research, and the remaining third on
private study and miscellaneous work; (b) that there is now an
improved staff/student ratio of about 1 : 8; (c) that promotion
through the grades of assistant lecturer, lecturer, senior lecturer,
reader and professor stems much more from research than
teaching; (d) that certain sections of staff suffer from shortage of
requisite research facilities.

Looking ahead, it may be forecast with confidence that if, as
predicted, the number qualified for higher education entry
doubles by about 1981, then new university-level institutions
may emerge. It may be that these will develop from existing non-
university higher educational centres (such as colleges of education and central institutions) or that various non-university
institutions will coalesce administratively with older universities
for degree purposes (the now familiar 'multiversity' or 'poly-
versity' concept). The latter alternative seems the more likely in
terms of practical politics for the universities and colleges of
education in view of the present Bachelor of Education degree
courses operated jointly by them on a combined academic and
professional basis.

The way ahead within the universities themselves has already
been pointed by the newer foundations, in using structures such

Students at universities in Scotland 1954–55 to 1969–70

Academic years

	Full-time first degree and first diploma students who entered for the first time(1)			Undergraduate population			Postgraduate population			Total population			
	Men	Women	Men & women	Men	Women	Men & women	Men	Women	Men & women	Men	Women	Men & women	
1954–55	2,280	1,080	3,360	9,093	3,562	12,655	1,222	266	1,488	10,315	3,828	14,143	1
1955–56	2,468	1,155	3,623	9,437	3,778	13,215	1,278	296	1,574	10,715	4,074	14,789	2
1956–57	2,612	1,217	3,829	9,792	3,982	13,774	1,286	281	1,567	11,078	4,263	15,341	3
1957–58	2,995	1,276	4,271	10,535	4,264	14,799	1,331	281	1,612	11,866	4,545	16,411	5
1958–59	3,154	1,277	4,431	11,108	4,418	15,526	1,371	279	1,650	12,479	4,697	17,176	4
1959–60	3,130	1,280	4,410	11,304	4,495	15,799	1,483	270	1,753	12,787	4,765	17,552	6
1960–61	3,241	1,457	4,698	11,891	4,747	16,638	1,592	299	1,891	13,483	5,046	18,529	7
1961–62	3,535	1,624	5,159	12,369	5,027	17,396	1,660	377	2,037	14,029	5,404	19,433	8
1962–63	3,673	1,725	5,398	12,875	5,445	18,320	1,832	421	2,253	14,707	5,866	20,573	9
1963–64	4,045	1,826	5,871	13,665	5,848	19,513	1,974	434	2,408	15,639	6,282	21,921	10
1964–65	4,830	2,524	7,354	15,303	7,195	22,498	2,221	564	2,785	17,524	7,759	25,283	11
1965–66	5,424	2,798	8,222	17,511	8,004	25,515	2,062	540	2,602	19,573	8,544	28,117	12
1966–67	5,371	2,865	8,326	18,152	8,640	26,792	2,319	637	2,956	20,471	9,277	29,748	13
1967–68	5,918	3,004	8,922	19,553	9,322	28,875	2,482	735	3,217	22,035	10,057	32,092	14
1968–69	6,028	3,012	9,040	20,558	9,734	30,292	2,721	796	3,517	23,279	10,530	33,809	15
1969–70(2)	6,171	3,240	9,411	21,430	10,088	31,518	2,566	814	3,380	23,996	10,902	34,898	16

(1) See Note (3).
(2) Provisional.

From: *Scottish Educational Statistics*, 1969.

Subject group of study of all full-time students
(i) At undergraduate level
(a) Men

At 31st December, 1968

	Education	Medicine, dentistry and health	Engineering and technology	Agriculture, forestry and veterinary science	Science	Social, administrative and business studies	Architecture and other professional and vocational subjects	Language, literature and area studies	Arts other than languages	Total	
Aberdeen	6	371	279	99	1,113	749	—	184	114	2,915	1
Dundee	—	444	283	—	366	507	—	9	17	1,626	2
Edinburgh	30	906	530	361	978	1,010	103	341	612	4,871	3
Glasgow	—	1,026	429	224	1,460	641	—	83	940	4,803	4
Heriot-Watt	—	75	945	—	292	266	—	—	—	1,578	5
St Andrews	—	111	—	—	540	93	—	213	231	1,188	6
Stirling	2	—	—	—	28	49	—	39	30	148	7
Strathclyde	—	100	1,552	—	649	848	249	31	—	3,429	8
Total Scotland	38	3,033	4,018	684	5,426	4,163	352	900	1,944	20,558	9
As percentage of total	0·2	14·8	19·5	3·3	26·4	20·3	1·7	4·4	9·5	100·0	10

(b) Women

Aberdeen	26	188	3	5	509	662	—	258	45	1,696	1
Dundee	—	139	3	—	133	218	—	19	9	521	2
Edinburgh	156	347	2	57	343	635	42	575	898	3,055	3
Glasgow	—	342	2	65	409	141	—	64	1,196	2,219	4
Heriot-Watt	—	64	1	—	38	81	—	—	—	184	5
St Andrews	—	38	—	—	227	80	—	352	237	934	6
Stirling	8	—	—	—	23	37	—	55	16	139	7
Strathclyde	—	91	22	—	120	615	88	50	—	986	8
Total Scotland	190	1,209	33	127	1,802	2,469	130	1,373	2,401	9,734	9
As percentage of total	2·0	12·4	0·3	1·3	18·5	25·4	1·3	14·1	24·7	100·0	10

(c) Men and women

Aberdeen	32	559	282	104	1,622	1,411	—	442	159	4,611	1
Dundee	—	583	286	—	499	725	—	28	26	2,147	2
Edinburgh	186	1,253	532	418	1,321	1,645	145	916	1,510	7,926	3
Glasgow	—	1,368	431	289	1,869	782	—	147	2,136	7,022	4
Heriot-Watt	—	139	946	—	330	347	—	—	—	1,762	5
St Andrews	—	149	—	—	767	173	—	565	468	2,122	6
Stirling	10	—	—	—	51	86	—	94	46	287	7
Strathclyde	—	191	1,574	—	769	1,463	337	81	—	4,415	8
Total Scotland	228	4,242	4,051	811	7,228	6,632	482	2,273	4,345	30,292	9
As percentage of total	0·8	14·0	13·4	2·7	23·9	21·9	1·6	7·5	14·3	100·0	10

From: *Scottish Educational Statistics, 1969*

Subject group of study of all full-time students

(ii) At postgraduate level

(a) Men

At 31st December, 1968

	Education	Medicine, dentistry and health	Engineering and technology	Agriculture, forestry and veterinary science	Science	Social, administrative and business studies	Architecture and other professional and vocational subjects	Language, literature and area studies	Arts other than languages	Total	
Aberdeen	69	14	15	43	92	29	—	13	15	290	1
Dundee	46	27	18	—	89	17	—	—	2	199	2
Edinburgh	72	42	51	63	308	129	76	115	103	959	3
Glasgow	83	38	39	9	206	70	15	28	24	512	4
Heriot-Watt	—	3	31	—	34	14	2	—	—	84	5
St Andrews	—	—	—	—	94	9	—	21	31	155	6
Stirling	2	—	5	—	15	12	—	1	3	38	7
Strathclyde	—	30	202	—	109	111	25	7	—	484	8
Total Scotland	272	154	361	115	947	391	118	185	178	2,721	9
As percentage of total	10·0	5·7	13·3	4·2	34·8	14·4	4·3	6·8	6·5	100·0	10

(b) Women

No.		1	2	3	4	5	6	7	8	9	Total
1	Aberdeen	50	1	—	5	20	19	—	6	7	108
2	Dundee	24	7	—	—	8	18	—	2	—	59
3	Edinburgh	53	15	—	5	52	80	7	57	39	308
4	Glasgow	79	16	—	—	28	17	5	12	7	164
5	Heriot-Watt	—	3	—	—	—	—	—	—	—	3
6	St Andrews	—	—	—	—	14	2	—	6	6	28
7	Stirling	1	—	—	—	4	—	—	—	—	5
8	Strathclyde	—	5	2	—	7	77	27	3	—	121
9	Total Scotland	207	47	2	10	133	213	39	86	59	796
10	As percentage of total	26·0	5·9	0·3	1·3	16·7	26·8	4·9	10·8	7·4	100·0

(c) Men and women

No.		1	2	3	4	5	6	7	8	9	Total
1	Aberdeen	119	15	15	48	112	48	—	19	22	398
2	Dundee	70	34	18	—	97	35	—	2	2	258
3	Edinburgh	125	57	51	68	360	209	83	172	142	1,267
4	Glasgow	162	54	39	9	234	87	20	40	31	676
5	Heriot-Watt	—	6	31	—	34	14	2	—	—	87
6	St Andrews	—	—	—	—	108	11	—	27	37	183
7	Stirling	3	—	5	—	19	12	—	1	3	43
8	Strathclyde	—	35	204	—	116	188	52	10	—	605
9	Total Scotland	479	201	363	125	1,080	604	157	271	237	3,517
10	As percentage of total	13·6	5·7	10·3	3·6	30·7	17·2	4·5	7·7	6·7	100·0

From: *Scottish Educational Statistics*, 1969

as schools of allied studies rather than faculties, and in aiming more at professional preparation in the subjects studied. One other trend is that some universities have moved from the typically Scottish 'common start and late differentiation' of Ordinary and Honours studies to the more typically English separation of the two. In this the oldest Scottish foundation in St Andrews is conservative by contrast with the increasingly cosmopolitan and internationally popular Edinburgh.

Since two types of first degree are available in Scottish universities, this principle should soon extend to the relatively new BEd degree in which the colleges of education are also involved. Until recently only an Ordinary degree was offered (details of which the reader will find below in the discussion of teacher training), perhaps because of initial uncertainty about the calibre and capability of the students involved. But all through the years since its inception in 1965 pressure has been mounting from staff (university and college) and students for the construction of a BEd Honours degree in a suitable range of special subjects. Evidence is available that a number of students amongst the BEd group (the writer's opinion is that this minority is growing annually as the BEd intake increases and attracts more and better students) would benefit from such an offer. From about 1970, serious discussion was begun in Aberdeen and Dundee on the form and structure of a five-year course (six years for modern languages, affected by foreign residence requirements) in a range of subjects; the first course started in Aberdeen in October 1972. In line with Scottish precedent, every student in his first two years will follow a pattern that leads to the Ordinary degree. Only in the third year will university 'bridging' courses be available for those considered good enough, leading to junior and senior Honours in the fourth and fifth years. This is to be welcomed as a step forward in motivating able school-leavers, who intend to teach, to take a course combining, it is hoped, the best of both worlds.

Trends in teacher education   The phrase 'teacher education' is used advisedly, since many factors have combined to make the narrow concept of 'training' a thing of the past for

Scottish teachers. The emphasis of the present day is on the teacher's emergence as a professional person who is also competent in the classroom.

In general, teacher education is a fast-changing field in the sense that it is growing in size and diversity, that control over it has passed from the Secretary of State to colleges and the General Teaching Council, that proposals for new courses are increasingly a common feature, and so forth. There are at present ten colleges of education. The colleges at Aberdeen, Dundee, Jordanhill in Glasgow and Moray House in Edinburgh have a full representative spread of all categories of Scottish teacher as shown on pp 112–13. The only exception to this is the category of physical education teacher, but in Jordanhill the only absent group is that of women physical education teachers, since their male counterparts are centralised in the Scottish School of Physical Education attached to the college. It should be stressed, especially for non-Scottish readers, that postgraduate teacher education is statutory in Scotland, and that the Scottish major colleges are fairly unusual internationally in combining it with undergraduate or non-graduate teacher education. The latter is catered for in most countries by the elementary teacher's college or normal school. In other words, it is legally necessary in Scotland (recently now also in England) for all teachers, including all graduates, to take a period of training before entry to the profession.

Of the six other colleges, Notre Dame in Glasgow and Craiglockhart in Edinburgh are for Roman Catholic women following any type of course; Callendar Park in Falkirk, Craigie in Ayr and Hamilton College take women and a few men non-graduates only; and Dunfermline College of Physical Education in Edinburgh takes women physical education teachers.

Since the Teachers (Training Authorities) (Scotland) Regulations of 1958, these colleges have had increased autonomy (as colleges of education) through the creation of governing bodies responsible over four-year periods (three years before 1967) for every conceivable aspect of the individual college's work in staffing, course content, research, finance and allied fields. The

Training of Teachers

All students in main courses in Colleges of Education leading to award of teaching qualifications

	Students who commenced training in session				Students in training in November			Students who successfully completed training in session			
	1967–68	1968–69	1969–70	1970–71 (provl.)	1968	1969	1970	1967–68	1968–69	1969–70	
Primary Qualification											
Honours graduates											
Men	5	11	12	17	12	13	17	5	11	11	1
Women	18	24	30	29	23	30	29	15	23	26	2
Men and Women	23	35	42	46	35	43	46	20	34	37	3
Ordinary graduates											
Men	30	19	23	28	18	20	28	30	17	21	4
Women	133	132	154	141	136	157	141	118	129	146	5
Men and Women	163	151	177	169	154	177	169	148	146	167	6
Non-graduates											
Men	293	283	288	280	545	765	754	18	13	243	7
Women	2,284	2,520	2,624	2,491	6,744	7,109	7,184	2,245	1,987	2,071	8
Men and Women	2,577	2,803	2,912	2,771	7,289	7,874	7,938	2,263	2,000	2,314	9
Total											
Men	328	313	323	325	575	798	799	53	41	275	10
Women	2,435	2,676	2,808	2,661	6,903	7,296	7,354	2,378	2,139	2,243	11
Men and Women	2,763	2,989	3,131	2,986	7,478	8,094	8,153	2,431	2,180	2,518	12
Secondary Qualification											
Honours graduates											
Men	296	342	387	421	342	390	421	282	323	367	13
Women	159	217	243	276	218	254	279	155	206	243	14
Men and Women	455	559	630	697	560	644	700	437	529	610	15
Ordinary graduates											
Men	264	294	304	346	293	306	346	237	272	287	16
Women	391	456	499	500	455	504	502	378	444	487	17
Men and Women	655	750	803	846	748	810	848	615	716	774	18
Non-graduates											
Men	275	286	289	297	514	515	532	257	262	260	19
Women	583	691	650	597	1,180	1,170	1,118	482	597	600	20
Men and Women	858	977	939	894	1,694	1,685	1,650	739	859	860	21
Total											
Men											

Category	No.										
Women	26	1	4	2	4	8	9	6	1	1	3
Men and Women	27	27	73	30	64	102	107	74	31	26	71
Ordinary graduates											
Men	28	8	12	43	48	15	29	91	7	9	45
Women	29	1	4	9	13	4	6	22	2	1	7
Men and Women	30	9	16	52	61	19	35	113	9	10	52
Non-graduates											
Men	31	170	161	114	130	357	335	244	155	159	116
Women	32	34	23	21	22	62	59	43	17	32	19
Men and Women	33	204	184	135	152	419	394	287	172	191	135
Total											
Men	34	204	242	185	218	466	462	403	192	193	229
Women	35	36	31	32	39	74	74	71	20	34	29
Men and Women	36	240	273	217	257	540	536	474	212	227	258
Bachelor of Education(2)(3)											
Men	37	38	46	60	74	154	206	223	—	18	41
Women	38	158	186	173	218	486	598	667	3	32	99
Men and Women	39	196	232	233	292	640	804	890	3	50	140
All Above Courses											
Honours graduates											
Men	40	327	422	427	478	448	501	506	317	359	446
Women	41	178	245	275	309	249	193	314	171	230	272
Men and Women	42	505	667	702	787	697	794	820	488	589	718
Ordinary graduates											
Men	43	302	325	370	422	326	355	465	274	298	353
Women	44	525	592	662	654	595	667	665	498	574	640
Men and Women	45	827	917	1,032	1,076	921	1,022	1,130	772	872	993
Non-graduates (including B.Ed.)											
Men	46	776	776	751	781	1,570	1,821	1,753	430	452	660
Women	47	3,059	3,420	3,468	3,328	8,472	8,936	9,012	2,747	2,648	2,789
Men and Women	48	3,835	4,196	4,219	4,109	10,042	10,757	10,765	3,177	3,100	3,449
Grand Total											
Men	49	1,405	1,523	1,548	1,681	2,344	2,677	2,724	1,021	1,109	1,459
Women	50	3,762	4,257	4,405	4,291	9,316	9,896	9,991	3,416	3,452	3,701
Men and Women	51	5,167	5,780	5,953	5,972	11,660	12,573	12,715	4,437	4,561	5,160

(1) With the exception of those in the Further Education qualification course, all the students in the Table are in full-time courses prior to employment as qualified teachers. The course for the Further Education Qualification is an in-service course consisting of two months' attendance at the College of Education, followed by ten months in teaching employment and a final two months in the College. The figures of students in training in November comprise all students who have entered the first period of College of Education attendance and have not left or successfully completed the second period.

(2) The Bachelor of Education course was inaugurated in session 1965–66. This course is of four years' duration.

(3) At Dundee College of Education all students taking Bachelor of Education degrees are enrolled initially in a Primary qualification course and have been counted under the latter only.

From: *Scottish Educational Statistics*, 1970

reader will remember that the evolution from church control to autonomy has in Scottish colleges been very different from the English college pattern, where to this day colleges, especially small ones, suffer from the disadvantages often accompanying denominational or indeed local authority status (regionalisation of local government in England may pull English colleges out of this position into a more satisfactory one akin to the Scottish). The large Scottish college is as near to university level in its composition as any institution of teacher education in the world, with the possible exception of university integrated teachers' colleges in the United States. This is especially true today since a portion of its student body consists of university matriculated undergraduates, and a sizable number of its staff are recognised as university teachers for the purposes of the BEd degrees.

Since 1958 staffs have had the right to participate in the oversight of all academic matters in the college in the so-called board of studies, which has an advisory function vis-à-vis the principal of the college, whose task it is to take final decisions. Recently, with the tremendous expansion of the college staffs, the trend has been to replace this unwieldy body with a policy committee consisting of all heads of department and an elected representation from the rest of the staff. Status of staff was also enhanced in 1967 by an entitlement to representation on the governing body of the college, along with teachers, local authority representatives, university members and all appropriate local and regional interests in education.

Though enjoying this degree of autonomy, the colleges of education are, in view of financial control by the Scottish Education Department, state institutions to a far greater degree than the universities. Centrally the Scottish Education Department allocates 75 per cent of annual finance and the new General Teaching Council (which in 1966 took over the supervision of college courses from the former Scottish Council for the Training of Teachers) maintains a watching brief over course content. But availability of finance as dictated by current national economic conditions is the only real curb on the Scottish college's individual freedom of action, since the General Teaching Council (although in theory entitled to veto inappropriate course content) in practice holds the reins loosely by comparison with the Scottish Council's pre-1966 policy and thus encourages the growth to autonomy begun in 1958.

It is also important to mention the 1967 Teachers (Colleges of Education) Regulations which have modified the basic 1958 position. A good example of how they have done this can be seen from the relative composition of the Aberdeen College of Education Governing Body in both years, as follows:

Representatives	*1958*		*1967*	
Aberdeen City Education Authority	2		2	
Association of County Councils	6		6	
Senate, Aberdeen University	3		4	[increase of one]
Teachers	7	⎧ 1 primary head 1 junior secondary head 1 senior secondary head 1 further education head ⎩ 3 others	7	⎧ instead of 1 junior secondary and 1 senior secondary head, 'two head teachers of secondary schools'
Education Committee, General Assembly, Church of Scotland	3		3	
In addition:				
Association of Directors of Education	–		1	
College of Education staff	–		6	⎧ principal, vice-principal and 4 lecturing staff

Thus, the most important change made at this time was in the introduction of a more adequately representative structure, and particularly of members of the colleges' own academic staff. But the term of service of governing bodies became one of four years instead of three, so that in 1971 the first of these reconstituted governing bodies completed service, and the life of the next ends in 1975.

There is a wide variety of courses provided in the colleges for teachers in primary and secondary schools and further education colleges (the whole range is available only in the four big colleges and the further education training is confined centrally to Jordanhill, Glasgow). All these courses lead to what have been officially termed, since the Teachers (Education, Training and Registration) (Scotland) Regulations of 1967,* (a) the Teaching Qualification (Primary Education), (b) the Teaching Qualification (Secondary Education) and (c) the Teaching Qualification (Further Education), after periods in college of varying length, dependent on prior entry levels. These courses tend to be subdivided into:

1. (for students following three/four year courses)
    (a) a three-year diploma course for primary teaching (women and a few men)
    (b) two-, three- or four-year course for technical subjects in secondary teaching (men)
    (c) four-year combined university and college course (men and women) for Bachelor of Education degree— secondary or primary (five/six years in future Honours course)
    (d) four-year 'diploma plus Froebel' course for primary infant stage (women)
    (e) three-year music diploma—secondary (a four-year course is under discussion)
2. (for students following one-year courses)
    (a) postgraduate (Honours)—secondary
    (b) postgraduate (Ordinary)—secondary
    (c) postgraduate (Ordinary)—primary
    (d) postdiploma (art, music and domestic science students from other colleges)—secondary

This is not a comprehensive list of all that happens in every college, but it gives a cross-section of the all-embracing coverage of the teacher education process by colleges in Scotland. In fact, some of the larger colleges have developed courses parallel to these for the training of youth leaders and social workers, so that

* These supersede the corresponding Regulations of 1965 on Education Training and Certification. The significant change to the term 'Registration' in 1967 is explained by the birth of the General Teaching Council in 1966 and the new requirement that teachers register with it.

some at least are diversified in function beyond the bounds of pure teacher education.

Let us refer back briefly to the above main programme of courses in the colleges of education and consider conditions for entry to them and the nationally recognised qualifications issuing from them. Course 1 (a) requires a full secondary education with an offering of four Higher passes, OR three Highers with two O Grades, OR two Highers and four O Grades—in each case Higher English and a pass in arithmetic/mathematics. Course 1 (b) for technical subjects starts from a wide variety of bases and experience levels, involving Higher National Diplomas, Higher SCE passes, industrial experience etc—the higher the initial level the shorter the course. Course 1 (c) except in Dundee which has a common initial diploma/BEd year, involves normal university entrance requirements. Course 1 (d) is essentially for highly successful three-year diploma women who wish to take in a fourth year the National Froebel Foundation certificate (there are allied non-NFF one- and two-term courses for nursery and infant teachers). Course 1 (e) needs almost the same as 1 (a) (ie two Highers and three O Grades) but also, naturally, tests of executant musical ability. On courses 2 (a) to (d) the level of entry is obviously degree, diploma, associateship or its equivalent from the university or central institution. The larger Scottish college is in any academic year an amalgam of one-year student populations from various other sources with those following a three/four year course entirely in college.

Most courses cover (a) teaching method, (b) teaching practice, and (c) the study of professional subjects, the most important being education and educational psychology. Such subjects as sociology of education are growing—and indeed pure sociology as contained in the main study programme of three-year diploma students among the range of options. If there is a major difference between the programmes for students 'from elsewhere' and the college's 'own students' it is in the greater emphasis in the latter case on the general education as well as professional preparation of the student.

Recent proposals for 'Associateships of the Colleges of

Education' recognising *four*-year secondary courses of different
sorts in colleges has met with some antagonism, chiefly on the
ground that this is a political manoeuvre to convert primary
teachers into secondary (eg in the case of three-year diploma
men) and to 'dilute' academic standards. So far the only teachers
to receive the designation ACE have been in the primary category
—those achieving National Froebel Foundation level. It will be
interesting in 1974, when men technical teachers complete the
first non-degree four-year courses for secondary qualification, to
see whether the old arguments prevail. They, and the growing
group of three-year diploma men students—who could con-
ceivably qualify for 'middle school' (ten to fourteen) teaching—
and possibly also the future emergence of four-year music and
drama diplomas will pose problems for the traditionalists.

A special word is called for on the BEd degree, perhaps the most
promising feature in Scottish teacher education. The example
of the Aberdeen degree, which is the oldest in Scotland (and indeed in Britain), will serve as an illustration, although the pattern
varies. In Aberdeen the student must in four years achieve a
minimum of seven passes (usual for a Scottish ordinary degree)
which must contain two academic subjects at ordinary class level,
education and educational psychology, one practical subject
(from music, art, physical education, drama etc—a special
Aberdeen feature) one pass at least at advanced level, and one
other. This, with methods and teaching practice throughout four
years, renders the whole a combined academic-professional
degree. It is from those who can achieve the required passes and
move at a faster than average pace, that the BEd Honours group
(mentioned above) will be drawn.

Among the student body of any college there is usually a
sizable group, on the whole highly motivated, who enter under
the Special Recruitment Scheme, operated to encourage mature
men and women to take up teaching as a career at a later stage
than is usual. These follow exactly the same courses to the same
levels as all the others, and constitute a welcome extra source of
students, though economic considerations now limit intake.

There is a present shortage of teachers, confined to—but

diminishing rapidly in—the secondary sector and in the central industrial belt. The central belt has indeed been driven to desperate expedients such as part-time and 'shift' schooling. Also there is a continuing 'turnover' of teachers, with a steady loss of married women, but with the prospect of a gradual return of the same group when their children are of primary school age. So far that return has been slow. There is also a current shortage in the maths/science area of the secondary schools as opposed to the arts subjects.

Three other facets of the current college scene are of interest. Firstly, in-service training for teachers already in the profession has been growing phenomenally for years, and is now organised under national and regional committees. The range of courses is increasing and the traditional summer vacation load is being spread over the session in evening, day, weekend and other courses run both by the colleges and the local authorities. Secondly, relationships between colleges and schools are gradually improving from the old irrational 'ivory tower' versus 'real battlefield' syndrome to a growing partnership in which college staff regularly teach in schools and teachers participate experimentally to a limited extent in teacher-tutor supervision of students in training. Lastly, in the colleges themselves, student participation in the decision structure is increasing healthily in a welter of committees where staff and students solve problems together.

If we cast a retrospective eye over the last fourteen years or so of Scottish teacher education (since the inception of the 'governing body phase'), we see the following developments. Staff and student numbers have exploded beyond expectation—in Aberdeen College, for instance, by about 150 per cent in the period 1961–71; Scottish colleges are large now by European standards, Jordanhill having in session 1970–1 over 3,000 students and 306 staff, Moray House 2,650 students and 180 staff, Aberdeen 1,600 students and 150 staff, Dundee 1,150 students and 126 staff. University graduate intake has risen steeply; courses have diversified, especially in Jordanhill and Moray House, this being the partial explanation of the above figures for these colleges.

The non-graduate three-year population has also greatly increased; the general proportion of men to women in all training courses is increasing slowly. New staff qualifications and promotion prospects have been noticeably affected by the presence of university staff on selection panels and the prospect of recognition for BEd teaching by the university.

The picture in about 1981 promises to be one of closer association with universities and greater prominence for the BEd degree; an increase in four-year courses of different kinds and the emergence of a situation in which four years becomes a desirable minimum for professional entry, which will mean the slow death of the three-year diploma. We shall expect to see the colleges preparing students for other professions as well as teaching, and expanding in-service courses leading to promoted posts. A new form of postgraduate training (which is still under discussion) may radically change the present 'one year after university' situation into a three-phase pattern consisting of (i) a period of basic orientation in college, (ii) a period of *'earning* and learning' in a local authority school and (iii) a second period in college for consolidation, discussion, self-improvement, and more advanced professional education leading to the full teaching qualification. There may also be a wider provision of specialist diplomas in creative/aesthetic subjects within the colleges.

THE TEACHER

What of the profession these students will enter? The reader will recall the various stages in Scottish educational history at which, through legislation, the professional status and security of tenure of the teacher was improved. In the 1970s we should achieve fully qualified staffing of the schools (this is so in primary now but not yet by any means in secondary), and a strongly protected professional tenure and rising status derived from a greater say in educational administration, teacher education, salary negotiation, and curriculum development.

The greatest advance achieved by the teaching profession in recent years has been the formation of the General Teaching Council, operational since 1966: a professional body designed to maintain control over future standards in Scottish teaching, and recently mentioned by UNESCO (*Educational Studies and Documents* No 3) as internationally outstanding. It is representatively composed of teachers in primary and secondary schools, further education establishments and colleges of education in fitting proportions. Its most important functions are to control entry to the profession (at the end of teacher training, student-teachers recommended as successful by the colleges of education now 'register' on payment of a fee with the GTC, instead of receiving 'certification' from the Secretary of State), to exercise discipline, via appropriate machinery, over any members of the profession who are considered personally, morally or otherwise unsuitable to continue in the profession, to maintain general oversight on teacher education, and to secure the disappearance of the un-certificated teacher from the Scottish educational scene. There are signs currently that England and Wales will follow suit—in fact Welsh teachers might have achieved this type of council years ago if they had not been tied, unlike the Scots, to the English system.

Salary structure   One other important feature of the professional scene is, of course, the salary structure and its power of attraction over prospective entrants to teaching. The reader will easily be able to judge how satisfactory or otherwise this is in Scotland by reference to the following outline.

Main Salary Scales (in force from April 1972)

Scale 1   £1,587–2,781 (10 years)

Honours graduates (and equivalent) in secondary schools and educational psychologists.

Scale 2   £1,401–2,442 (12 years)

Teachers in *secondary* schools as follows: ordinary graduates, teachers of art, teachers of speech and drama, certain teachers of commerce and music.

Teachers of technical subjects with certain supplementary qualifications.

Teachers of domestic science (Group III or equivalent).

In addition, holders of the new Diploma in Technical Subjects for which courses were introduced in October 1970 will be entitled to be paid on Scale 2 provided that they are employed in secondary schools.

Scale 3   £1,227–2,211 (12 years)

1. Teachers in *primary* schools holding the qualifications listed in Scale 2 above.

2. Teachers in *secondary* schools as follows: teachers of physical education; certain teachers of technical subjects and music.

3. Teachers of practical and aesthetic subjects in *secondary* schools as follows:

    Certain teachers of technical subjects, music, agriculture and horticulture who are not entitled to be paid on Scale 1 or 2.

    Teachers of domestic science holding the Group 1 Diploma or the Group II Diploma or the Diploma in Domestic Science instituted in session 1967–8.

    Certain teachers awarded the Teacher's Technical Certificate under Article 47 (bb) of the Training Regulations of 1931.

4. Women teachers in *primary* schools whose courses of training, leading to the award of a Teaching Qualification (Primary Education) *and* an infants mistress or nursery school endorsement, extended to not less than four years.

Scale 3A   £1,164–2,190 (14 years)

Teachers of practical and aesthetic subjects and certain teachers holding a Teaching Qualification (Primary Education) *and* Teaching Qualification (Secondary Education) continuing to serve in *primary* schools. These are teachers who hold qualifications referred to under scale 3 (2) above.

Scale 3B   £1,164–2,037 (14 years)

Teachers of practical and aesthetic subjects and certain teachers holding a Teaching Qualification (Primary Education) and a Teaching Qualification (Secondary Education) continuing to serve in *primary* schools.

Scale 4   £1,164–2,022 (14 years)

1. Teachers awarded a Teaching Qualification (Primary Education) as a result of a course at a college of education extending to not less than three years.

2. Teachers of pratical and aesthetic subjects in *primary* schools. These are teachers of domestic science (Group I or II or equivalent), teachers of music with a single qualification, teachers of technical subjects with no approved additional qualifications and certain teachers awarded the Teachers' Technical Certificate under Article 47 (bb) of the Training Regulations of 1931.

3. Teachers of practical and aesthetic subjects in primary schools who hold the qualifications referred to under Scale 3 (2).

The above are the main relevant scales as from 1972, applying to teachers currently emerging into the Scottish, as opposed to the English, profession; responsibility allowances are, of course, added to these for promoted posts according to size of school. These scales are fixed by the Secretary of State after consultation with the Scottish Joint Council for Teachers' Salaries. This council for a short time during 1964 contained representatives of all three Scottish teachers' organisations, with due regard to their size; but the Scottish Schoolmasters' Association, after a legal battle successfully waged to gain entry to the council, was excluded by the Secretary of State for refusal to keep its discussions confidential. It is still the case that teachers have a majority, however, over the local authority members of the council. No doubt the machinery will undergo change.

Superannuation is contributory, 6 per cent of salary being paid by the teacher and 7·5–8 per cent by the employing authority, the age at which the teacher's superannuable service ends being seventy, although sixty with at least thirty years service (with special arrangements for married women) usually qualifies for retirement allowance. This retirement allowance normally has two elements: pension and lump sum. The method of calculation is this: (i) pensionable salary is deemed to be the average of that received in the last three years of service; (ii) actual allowance is (a) pension = one-eighteenth of pensionable salary × number of 'years and days of service' to a maximum of forty-five years, *plus* (b) lump sum = one-thirtieth of pensionable salary × years plus days of service from service entry until 30 September 1956 and/or three-eightieths of pensionable salary × years plus days of service from 1 October 1956 to retirement—also to a limit of forty-five years. Actuarially-minded readers will no doubt be able to estimate the value of this scheme. In addition there is a widows' and children's scheme to which all *new* men teachers contribute 2 per cent of salary (although not all those serving since before its introduction in 1965 do so), and a dependants' scheme to which men and women alike can contribute if they wish.

Unions   Earlier mention was made of the three teachers' organisations—the Scottish teachers' trade unions. These are: (i) the Educational Institute of Scotland, of 125 years standing and containing 75 per cent of Scottish teachers of all categories; its voice is the *Scottish Educational Journal*, dedicated from its foundation to the advancement of Scottish education in general and teachers in particular, and to professional reunification—it carries considerable weight with the government in matters of policy; (ii) the Scottish Secondary Teachers' Association, its title indicating that it was (in 1947) a splinter group concerned about the submergence of secondary teachers' interests in a 'primary majority'; (iii) the Scottish Schoolmasters' Association, an all-male body dedicated to the safeguarding of men teachers' interests, formed in 1933. All three have a complex committee structure, and are grouped in local, regional and central executive patterns. Late in 1970, rumours were abroad about the possibility of a merger between EIS and SSTA, but these came to nothing since the SSTA claimed that the EIS had given publicity to the idea without prior inter-union consultation, and that no such merger could happen until adequate safeguards had been constructed for the interests of minority categories of teachers.

Status   It is difficult, even with such a situation as has been described, to estimate the status of the contemporary teacher in Scotland. Certainly, the parish school tradition of the past guaranteed a high regard in the rural areas—which still exists. But in a largely urbanised and industrialised society, where education competes for its trained manpower with other employing sources, and where the impersonality of the urban school situation and ingrained anti-education attitudes of some areas militate against status, new criteria are needed. These are to be found in salary levels, level and length of training, qualifications, the extent to which policy takes teacher opinion into account, and GTC-type control of the profession, as well as in increasing teacher-parent contact which increases sympathy and understanding towards the education process and the teacher's job.

A final comment, and a fair one, might well be that the sector of education we have just examined is perhaps the most important of the whole system, since it is on higher education in general and teacher education in particular that the quality of the personnel who operate the system depends.

6

From Arthur's Seat

THE native of Edinburgh has one tremendous advantage not always available to other urban dwellers. He has in the centre of his city a minor mountain from which in his more leisured moments he can see his city whole, realise its present extent and something of its historical development—and note those areas where the future is already taking shape. It is a revealingly different viewpoint from that enjoyed by an observer positioned in Princes Street, High Street—or even at the Scottish Office.

As a Scot all too prone, like most of his colleagues, to forget the Arthur's Seat view of Scottish education while immersed in its everyday ground-level business, the writer intends to use this last chapter as a vantage point, for Scot and non-Scot alike to view the system. The educational panorama, too, has in it something of the past, a great deal of the present, and indications for the future.

THE PAST

The combined effects of 400 years of reasonably continuous development in a small country with a conscious pattern and direction of schooling, the direct impact of relatively numerous (for a small country) universities upon the lives of a rural society and the typically Scottish hard-headed evaluation of the success of the educated in society are shown even now in an obsession with academic values and a continued, sometimes inappropriate, respect for the university degree. This causes the primary teacher to be still a little anxious about the trend towards a wider curriculum resulting from the removal of primary-secondary selection. It arouses suspicion in Scottish teachers' organisations about proposals to introduce trained teachers into the younger years of secondary by any path other than that which begins with graduate status. In tertiary education, it means that colleges of education and other non-university higher education institutions tend to be thought of as on a lower level than the university, even in this post-Robbins era. And the attitudes prevalent on the status of graduate and non-graduate teacher leave much to be desired.

But on the credit side the rural school pattern built up so carefully has generated greater equality of opportunity and easier availability of schooling for the rural child than in most other advanced countries. The geographical character of the country combined with a society much less class-structured than the English have eased transition to modern secondary provision (as opposed to curriculum reform). Scottish teacher-training history has produced the regional college, and the possibility of a united profession while other systems still struggle. A school entry age of five has ensured a progressive and altogether admirable school provision for a stage in which other countries are making desperate attempts to provide for the disadvantaged. The traditional insistence on the 'three Rs' in the past is the best guarantee against the danger of essential basic skills being lost while equally desirable curricular development is introduced. Scotland's academic past will ensure that any worthwhile comprehensive secondary school of the future, while catering for a varied range of ability, will also maintain its drive for excellence over a wide curricular spectrum.

THE PRESENT

If we search for the frontiers, the issues and the problems of the present day, we find a system increasingly characterised by partnership at many levels. Teachers co-operate more now with headmaster in curriculum development, and with colleagues in teachers' centres; HM Inspectors fill more and more a 'curriculum advice' role in conference with headmasters, teachers and college lecturers. College staffs experiment in more effective training of student teachers through the help of experienced teachers. The teaching profession has a modern role in local authority administration, and in the governing of colleges of education. And perhaps most significantly, the colleges of education are forging links in all directions—with universities in the BEd degree, with the SED in sponsored research, with schools in curriculum development as well as in training, with local authorities in the provision of in-service training for teachers, and so on.

In common with many other countries, increasing urbanisation in Scotland is focusing much attention on what might be called the lower fringe of compulsory schooling, the clamant need for expansion of nursery schooling especially deprived areas. Immigrants in the Glasgow area also pose problems. In the 'upper fringe' of compulsory schooling, the recent raising of the school-leaving age still causes much educational discussion. There is less anxiety over secondary teacher shortage, but much controversy over proposals from the Scottish Education Department on reorganised postgraduate training of teachers. Occasionally the proposal made a few years ago by the college of education principals for a four-year secondary associateship of the colleges is disinterred. Much curriculum development work takes place on the initiative of the Scottish Education Department and the local authorities, and there is close examination of the implications of the new concurrence of the leaving age and the O Grade examination. All this also implies that not until this problem has been satisfactorily dealt with—and that may be some years ahead—can time, money and effort be devoted to the 'lower fringe' of the system to the national extent desirable.

Certain emergent areas of school curriculum cause discussion and, in some cases, controversy. Modern foreign language and new mathematics are established growth points in primary schools, the first lagging in pace through lack of suitably qualified staff but gaining ground nevertheless, and the second developing quickly because of a wealth of interested discussion and experimentation by teachers (encouraged by some very fine in-service course provision in the colleges of education). In secondary school, anxiety still grips teachers over the suitability, extent and indeed possibility of mixed-ability class teaching in the lower years—and some real problems are met, such as the provision in the remoter rural areas of French for a full range of lower secondary classes. Also in the forefront of discussion is the exact nature of the counselling and guidance to be given within the Scottish secondary by the rapidly growing band of teachers at present being pressed by their local authorities and the Scottish Education Department to take up such posts of responsibility. Here, comparative information on practice in the United States and Scandinavia is a relevant topic for consideration. There is some disagreement on the future form and content of moral education in schools, particularly at secondary level, its exact relationship in the context of Scottish educational development with religious education, and uncertainty as to the choice of teachers to undertake it. The publication of the Millar Report on Religious Education and Moral Education in Scotland brings this to a head (see p 134) and future years will probably be characterised by fierce controversy among the teachers facing its challenge. Sex education does not yet find favour in all quarters, but is increasing rapidly in some schools, especially under the influence of some very well-produced television series usable by teachers. There is not, as in Sweden, anything like a nationally planned curriculum as yet. Not exactly controversial, but rather well accepted is the current appearance in the secondary school of new subjects necessary in the context of modern society; the best example of this is the growth of economics.

In the area of school building and design, interesting things are also happening, especially in the gradual appearance of (and general satisfaction so far with) various forms of the open-plan primary school, and the design of large new purpose-built comprehensive secondary schools (one very recently in Lanarkshire) inclusive of youth facilities, community centres, improved amenities for teaching staff and modern provision for audiovisual and library resource centres. It should perhaps be added that separate infant-stage schools for the five to seven group have also been educationally worthwhile, as in Aberdeen City.

Teacher education, too, has its frontiers and its controversies.

I

Present issues could be described as follows: the construction of a more effective and more attractive system of postgraduate training; adaptation of the structure of the BEd degree, and the addition of an Honours 'arm' to it: the emergence of four-year forms of teacher training in college and future associateships; much criticism of the academic content of the three-year diploma course; current experimental work in Stirling University on micro-teaching, and indeed the whole phenomenon of Stirling University as a centre of teacher education most atypical in Scotland; controversial trends in college staff appointments, stressing the academic perhaps more than the professional qualification; the emerging partnership between the schools and the colleges in tutoring for student teachers. Teacher education is obviously to an increasing extent within the orbit of the university, the main question being how strong the gravitational pull of the university will become.

From pre-service we come to in-service education of teachers. Present trends here can be described as a vast increase in the numbers of teachers involved, the development of the 'in-service habit', and a tentative development of courses in school business management and administration for future head teachers and other holders of newly created responsibility posts. If there is any problem, it is in the added burden thus placed on college staffs, and a detectable feeling among teachers that in-service should be timed to occur during the school session (the staffing gap to be filled by student teachers temporarily) rather than during summer vacation.

In educational administration and planning there are certain undocumented but none the less real issues at the time of writing which may be of importance. One of these is that in the urban area, the 'zone principle' of planned secondary school catchment areas is tending, no matter how careful the planners are in providing a social cross-section for the school, to run into difficulties. The parents able to pay for a private house in a suburban residential area are moving increasingly to the zones they consider 'desirable' and thus creating what could be described as an east-west polarisation of 'good' and 'bad' schools.

This raises doubts about the ultimate desirability of a one-tier 'orthodox' secondary system in the urban area.

Also in the sphere of administration, there is a mixed reception for the government's White Paper on Re-organisation of Local Government. The Orkney and Shetland Islands have received recognition of their feeling of separateness in a proposed degree of autonomy, and recently the Western Isles have shown a unanimous desire to be given status similar to Orkney and Shetland. But the 'Kingdom of Fife' with its identifiable unity of feeling is faced with the prospect of being dismembered for economic reasons. Concern is also expressed about the size, potential dominance and impersonality of the West Region and its lion's share of Scottish population.

THE FUTURE

Here, of course, we begin to speculate, but it is possible to make reasonable projections on the basis of present trends in education in Scotland, or at least to make reasonable guesses about main possible alternatives.

Almost certainly the new curricular offerings in mathematics, science and modern languages will take a firmer hold in primary schools. More teachers with a specialist leaning will find a place there, especially in the upper years, and there will be a steady increase towards a graduate primary-teaching force via avenues existing at the moment, but also via in-service courses, as now offered by Dundee College, and through the Open University. More head teachers of primary schools will have taken prerequisite management training, and it is likely that more men will be employed in the upper primary than at present. If anything comes of the Stirlingshire experiment with 'middle school' (scheduled to begin in 1973) we may expect to see corresponding adaption in teaching qualification requirements; a use of several categories of teachers in this ten-to-fourteen range; primary-secondary transition problems eased, new responsibility posts created in such schooling patterns and so on. But the greatest obstacle to overcome here will be conservative opposition to the admission of non-graduates to secondary school. On the other hand, the possible achievement of an all-graduate profession may cause middle schools to emerge. In the field of design, the open plan school mentioned earlier will probably be extensively used.

Secondary trends are likely, as is usual in Scotland, to take much the same path, but a few years later than primary. Certainly, design of secondary schools already foreshadows the future in its tendency towards 'campus spread', in purpose-built subject areas, information storage and retrieval services and the like. Mixed-ability class organisation will inevitably result in expanded production of teaching and resource materials centrally or regionally (eg under the auspices of post-Wheatley local authorities). There will probably be increasing flexibility of courses in upper secondary, and therefore the need for an effective and efficiently trained force of counsellors; the computer will be necessary for the even more complex timetabling. Headmasters themselves, like their primary colleagues, will require management training in policy and decision-making in the centralised and enlarged Scottish secondary school of the future. The grooming of candidates for promotion as in industry and the armed forces has been increasingly within the realm of possibility, and the recent choice of Moray House College for this function holds promise for the growth of a 'staff college' in Scotland.

Whether or not we ever have upper secondary schools in Scotland depends on the emergence or non-emergence of the middle school. Even if 'no sich animal' as the upper secondary evolves, the growth of the post-compulsory population is inevitably going to cause changes like those already taking place in the English sixth-form college, American senior high school, or Swedish gymnasium—new forms of democratic organisation such as school councils must appear and new subjects (sociology, politics, education, psychology) will also become normal. It is also conceivable that in the long term there may be some form of structural unification of separate upper secondary institutions, but in the shorter term linkage and transfer between schools and colleges of further education, their pupils, courses and staff are almost with us in Scotland.

What changes are there likely to be in the area of higher and teacher education? Already in Glasgow and Edinburgh non-university centres have reached university status, so that universities have increased numerically. But it is difficult to foresee a further 'joining of the club' by central institutions and colleges of education on any great scale. This is not just because it would make the cities top heavy with universities, but because their present linkage with existing universities through BEd and other degree courses seems to suggest a future federal or 'multiversity' pattern, especially in cities of the size of Aberdeen and Dundee. It seems probable that the future of teacher education lies in joining other professions under the general 'umbrella' of a university, with special status as a school, or university college, of education. The traditional Scottish attitude of respect for everything with a university label, irrational though it is, may be a strong factor to be reckoned with in decisions on the future of this sector. It would not be the first time, internationally speaking, that considerations of national status have featured either subtly or blatantly in hard-headed proposals for reform (the current extension of academic status names, such as 'sixth form' into 'sixth-form college' in England, and of 'gymnasium' into 'new gymnasium' in Sweden—is an example of this).

A number of other issues in the higher education scene are worth mentioning here: the possibility, after local government reorganisation, of pressure for a 'Highland University' or other forms of higher education facilities in Inverness (already Aberdeen College of Education has an interest in possible extension of its work there); the desirability of more emphasis on the study of education for undergraduates in arts, science and social science courses, especially as the current shortage of jobs in advertising/communications and industry is re-routing graduates to the state sector as potential teachers. This in turn seems to promise an explosive future for the colleges of education, but may have, if the trend is permanent, grave implications for university policy on future numbers at entry stage. Much under discussion are the increasing use of television and technology in higher education, the expansion of Open University studies and the eventual addition to teacher supply from the Open University as its degrees are to be acceptable for postgraduate programmes in colleges of education.

In administration, the new regions may be seen (i) as authorities which will regard educational planning as something to be closely integrated with 'overall socio-economic planning', and (ii) as power centres in education, promoting special educational needs in all areas of their territory within the context of national directives, catering especially, perhaps, for the equalisation of rural and urban education. In finance, greater control from the centre is very likely, but local authorities of the kind planned will probably have strong regional autonomy in the application of finance received.

There are social problems which promise to impinge upon educational institutions of the future. One of the most urgent of these is the abuse of drugs (becoming part of the Scottish scene in the 1970s) and the part schools and colleges will play in combating it.* Increase in crime and industrial unrest are two major trends which will necessitate greater concern with moral education. Some perfectly legitimate social trends also, such as earlier marriage and the lowering of the voting age to eighteen, imply greater concern with education in civics, while the growth of leisure time in an affluent society will force the schools to rethink and redirect plans for leisure training.

It is, of course, possible that, from 'Arthur's Seat' our view of the future has been distorted in places by 'bad visibility'. But we can claim a fair degree of accuracy and objectivity. We have seen Scottish education in the early 1970s as a thriving growth, with deep (and for the most part healthy) roots in the past, some fairly clear lines of evolution, and many suggestions of interesting and attractive things to come.

---

* Millar Report, March 1972 (*Moral and Religious Education in Scottish Schools*). Its main recommendations are (1) a Certificate of Sixth Year Studies examination (but none at 'O' or 'H' Grade) in Religious Studies, (2) training, qualification and use of specialist teachers in schools, (3) curriculum developments under the Consultative Committee on the Curriculum, (4) thematic and problem-linked religious and moral education, and (5) encouragement of moral responsibility by simulated situations.

Bibliography

Selected general publications

Aberdeen College of Education. *Education in the North*, magazine, Vol I: Special Education (1971)

Benn, C., and Simon, B. *Half Way There*, report on the British Comprehensive School Reform (Maidenhead, Berkshire, McGraw Hill 1970)

Hunter, S. L. *The Scottish Educational System* (Oxford, Pergamon Press 1968; second edition 1972)

Kerr, A. J. C. *Schools of Scotland* (Glasgow, Maclellan 1962)

Knox, H. M. *Two Hundred and Fifty Years of Scottish Education* (Edinburgh, Oliver & Boyd 1953)

Morgan, A. *Rise and Progress of Scottish Education* (Edinburgh, Oliver & Boyd 1927)

Nisbet, J. D., and Kirk, G. (ed). *Scottish Education Looks Ahead* (Edinburgh, Chambers 1969). Useful for information on many aspects of Scottish education since essays are contributed by specialists in many fields

Official publications

Committee on Higher Education. *Higher Education*, Robbins Report, including Appendices (London, HMSO 1963)

Public Schools Commission. *Second Report*, Volume 3: Scotland (London, HMSO 1970)

Scottish Certificate of Education Examination Board. Circulars 2 and 3; CSYS and Examinations conference report (Edinburgh, HMSO 1968 and 1970)

Scottish Education Department. *Education in Scotland in 1969*, Annual Blue book (Edinburgh, HMSO 1970) and the 1970 version when available

Education of Handicapped Pupils (Edinburgh, HMSO 1955)

From School to Further Education, Brunton Report (Edinburgh, HMSO 1963)

The Post-4th Year Examination Structure (Edinburgh, HMSO 1964)

Primary Education in Scotland (Edinburgh, HMSO 1966)

Raising the School Leaving Age (Edinburgh, HMSO 1966)

Re-organisation of Secondary Education on Comprehensive Lines, Circular 600 (Edinburgh, HMSO 1965)

Scottish Educational Statistics 1969 (Edinburgh, HMSO 1970) and the 1970 version when available

UNESCO. *Educational Studies and Documents*, No 3 (London, HMSO 1971)

University Grants Committee. *University Teaching Methods*, Hale Report (London, HMSO 1964)

Acknowledgements

The task of writing this book has been greatly eased by many and varied forms of help from others. In particular, the initial encouragement to contribute to this series was given by Dr M. D. Stephens of Liverpool University; Mr G. S. Osborne, Vice-Principal of Aberdeen College of Education, was kind enough to help eliminate inaccuracy, and Miss Patricia Sim to undergo the prolonged labour of MS typing.

For any qualities which may be thought to exist in the end product, credit is due to the guidance and co-operation of all concerned on the staff of David & Charles.

Should the reader harbour any adverse thoughts, let him direct them at the author alone.

I. R. F.

Index

139